Y0-AER-511

NELSON Language ARTS

TIMES TO SHARE

Caren Cameron

Maureen Dockendorf

Betty Eades

Barb Eklund

Christine Finochio

Ruth Hay

Sharon Jeroski

Eugene Mazur

Mary McCarthy

Wayne McNanney

Maureen Skinner

Chris Worsnop

Senior Program Consultant

Jennette MacKenzie

 I(T)P Nelson

an International Thomson Publishing company

Toronto • Albany • Bonn • Boston • Cincinnati • Detroit • London • Madrid • Melbourne
Mexico City • New York • Pacific Grove • Paris • San Francisco • Singapore • Tokyo • Washington

Grade 4 Reviewers:
Lynn Archer
New Westminster, British Columbia
Joyce Billinkoff
Winnipeg, Manitoba
Kerry Black
Calgary, Alberta
Faye Brownbridge
Calgary, Alberta
Mady Davidson
Winnipeg, Manitoba
Maureen Dockendorf
Port Moody, British Columbia
Linda Doody
Clarenville, Newfoundland
Carol Germyn
Calgary, Alberta
Charlotte Henryk
Regina, Saskatchewan
Phyllis Hildebrandt
Ste. Anne, Manitoba
Debra Huitema
Calgary, Alberta
Cheryl Lemire
Calgary, Alberta
Toni Marasco
Calgary, Alberta
Shawn Moynihan
Guelph, Ontario
Linda Nosbush
Prince Albert, Saskatchewan
Marilyn Raman
Winnipeg, Manitoba
Heather Weber
Whitby, Ontario
Shauneen Pete-Willett
Saskatoon, Saskatchewan
Wayne Williams
Clarenville, Newfoundland

Equity Consultant:
Ken Ramphal

I(T)P® International Thomson Publishing
The ITP logo is a trademark under licence
www.thomson.com

Published by
I(T)P® Nelson
A division of Thomson Canada Limited, 1998
1120 Birchmount Road
Scarborough, Ontario M1K 5G4
www.nelson.com

Printed and bound in Canada

1 2 3 4 5 6 7 8 9 0 / ML/ 7 6 5 4 3 2 1 0 9 8

Canadian Cataloguing in Publication Data

Main entry under title:

Nelson language arts 4

ISBN 0-17-607524-0 (v. 2 : bound)
ISBN 0-17-606607-1 (v. 2 : pbk.)
Contents: [2] Times to Share

1. Readers (Elementary). I. Cameron, Caren, 1949–   .

PE1121.N434 1997   428.6   C97-930958-1

Project Team: Angela Cluer, Mark Cobham, Daryn Dewalt, Kathleen ffolliott, Susan Green, Julie Greener, John McInnes, Allan Moon, Ken Phipps, June Reynolds, Elizabeth Salomons, Theresa Thomas, Jill Young

TABLE OF CONTENTS

Unit 2 *How It Works*

74

Unit 3 *Stories Well Told* 120

Unit 1: *Times to Share*

Think about all the people you spend time with: your family, your friends, your classmates. Who else do you spend time with? What do you talk about? What do you do?

Other people are very important in our lives. In this unit, you will read about people who share ideas, dreams, and problems. You will see how some people use language to communicate. You will

- read stories and poems to see how others share and work together
- read about special relationships with friends and family
- see how using language in the right way can help you get along better with others
- use reading tips to help you understand the meaning of what you read
- work together in a group to share tasks and encourage each other
- make a group photo essay

7

ALL *the* PLACES *to* LOVE

Written by Patricia MacLachlan
Illustrated by Mike Wimmer

READING TIP

Think about your experiences

Brainstorm a list of all your favourite places around your
home. Think about why you like these places. Read to find
out about the favourite places of the family in this story.

On the day I was born
My grandmother wrapped me in a blanket
      made from the wool of her sheep.

She held me up in the open window
So that what I heard first was the wind.
What I saw first were all the places to love:
The valley,
The river falling down over rocks,
The hilltop where the blueberries grew.

My grandfather was painting the barn,
And when he saw me he cried.
He carved my name—ELI—
On a rafter beside his name
And Grandmother's name
And the names of my papa and mama.

8

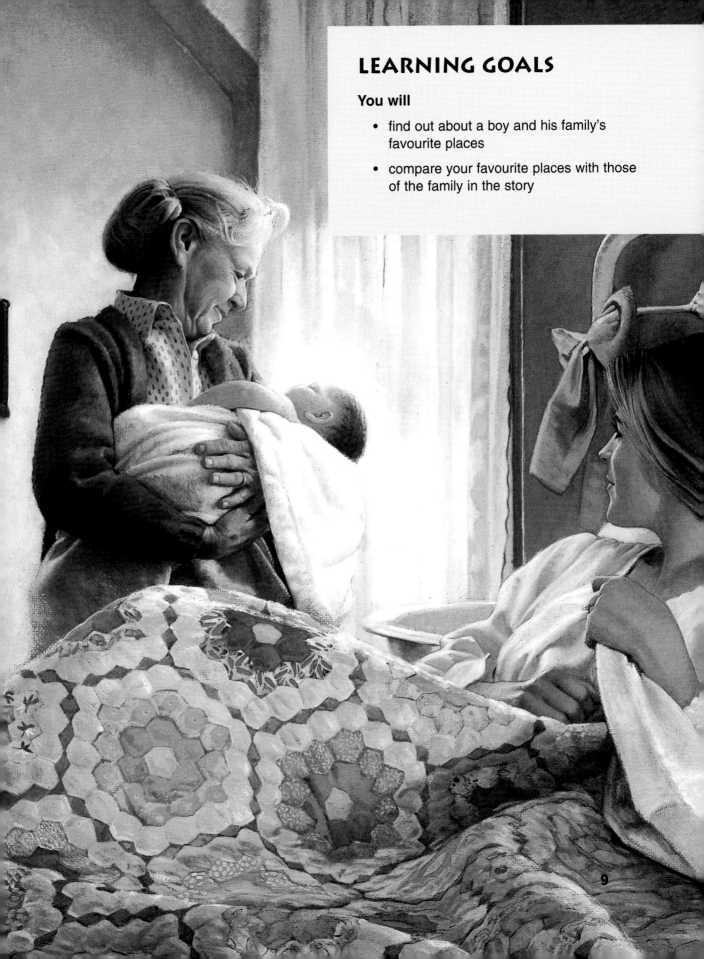

LEARNING GOALS

You will

- find out about a boy and his family's favourite places
- compare your favourite places with those of the family in the story

9

Mama carried me on her shoulders before I could walk,
Through the meadows and hay fields.
The cows watched us and the sheep scattered;
The dogs ran ahead, looking back with sly smiles.
When the grass was high
Only their tails showed.

When I was older, Papa and I plowed the fields.
Where else is soil so sweet? he said.
Once Papa and I lay down in the field, holding hands,
And the birds surrounded us:
Raucous black grackles, redwings,
Crows in the dirt that swaggered like pirates.
When we left, Papa put a handful of dirt in his pocket.
I did too.

My grandmother loved the river best
        of all the places to love.
That sound, like a whisper, she said;
Gathering in pools
Where trout flashed like jewels in the sunlight.
Grandmother sailed little bark boats downriver to me
With messages.
I Love You Eli, one said.

We jumped from rock to rock to rock,
Across the river to where the woods began,
Where bunchberry grew under the pine-needle path
And trillium bloomed.
Under the beech tree was a soft, rounded bed
        where a deer had slept.
The bed was warm when I touched it.

When spring rains came and the meadow turned to marsh,
Cattails stood like guards, and killdeers called.
Ducks nested by marsh marigolds,
And the old turtle—his shell all worn—
No matter how slow,
Still surprised me.

Sometimes we climbed to the place Mama loved best,
With our blueberry buckets and a chair for my
        grandmother:
To the blueberry barren where no trees grew—
The sky an arm's length away;
Where marsh hawks skimmed over the land,
And bears came to eat fruit,
And wild turkeys left footprints for us to find,
Like messages.
Where else, said my mama, *can I see the sun rise on one side*
And the sun set on the other?

My grandfather's barn is sweet-smelling
        and dark and cool;
Leather harnesses hang like paintings against old wood;
And hay dust floats like gold in the air.
Grandfather once lived in the city,
And once he lived by the sea;
But the barn is the place he loves most.
Where else, he says, *can the soft sound of cows chewing*
Make all the difference in the world?

Today we wait, him sitting on a wooden-slat chair
And me on the hay,
Until, much later, my grandmother holds up a small bundle
        in the open window,
Wrapped in a blanket made from the wool of her sheep,
And my grandfather cries.

Together
We carve the name SYLVIE in the rafter
Beside the names of Grandfather and Grandmother,
And my mama and papa,
And me.

My sister is born.

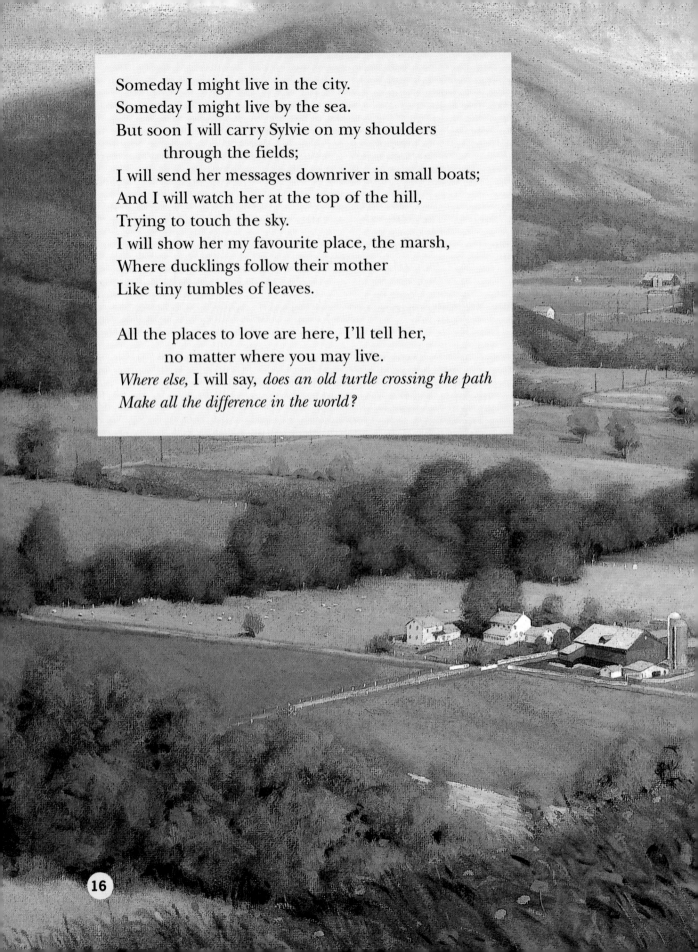

Someday I might live in the city.
Someday I might live by the sea.
But soon I will carry Sylvie on my shoulders
        through the fields;
I will send her messages downriver in small boats;
And I will watch her at the top of the hill,
Trying to touch the sky.
I will show her my favourite place, the marsh,
Where ducklings follow their mother
Like tiny tumbles of leaves.

All the places to love are here, I'll tell her,
        no matter where you may live.
Where else, I will say, *does an old turtle crossing the path*
Make all the difference in the world?

AFTER YOU READ

Write a summary sentence

Each person in the story had a favourite place. They told why they liked it by using a simple sentence that started with "*Where else....*" Write a "where else" sentence that tells about your favourite place.

Together Is Better

The Tiny Kite

Written by Maxine Trottier
Illustrated by Al Van Mil

Once there was a small boy named Eddie Wing. He lived in a city of tall hills by a bay. His home was above a flower stall and each day he helped his parents at their work. His mother and father loved him very much, but they worried over him. From the moment Eddie got up until the moment he went to sleep, he thought of nothing but kites.

Like most of the people on their street, the Wing family was very poor. Though Eddie could dream of fine silk kites, there was no money for even the smallest paper kite. So, Eddie made do with his dreams.

Every day after the flower stall was closed, Eddie Wing would climb to the top of the city's highest hills. There, he would run through the grass holding an imaginary string in one hand. With the other hand he would pull on the invisible cord and urge a kite that only he could see up into the cold, blue sky. At first the other children laughed. Then they stopped to watch. Finally one day, they all ran behind Eddie, cheering for the kite that they could *almost* see.

# of Eddie Wing

LEARNING GOALS

You will

- read how a young boy and an old man help make each other's dreams come true
- put yourself in the main character's place

Eddie's favourite event of the year was The Festival of Kites. He had watched the competitions ever since he could remember. And ever since he could remember, a prize had been offered by Old Chan. Chan was the most prosperous man in the whole neighbourhood. He owned a large restaurant and a store. Everyone who passed him in the street stopped and bowed.

Of course, Old Chan no longer worked in his restaurant. He only sat outside the store and thought about the days before he was so important—when he was a little boy in China with his whole life ahead of him.

In those days he had his own dream. He had wanted to be a poet. But when his family sailed across the sea to make a new start, there was no time for poetry. Chan's dream lay hidden like a tiny seed that has been planted, but never watered.

It was Chan who made up the test for The Festival of Kites each summer. One year it was for the fastest kite. Another time it was for the kite with the longest tail.

No one knew from year to year what challenge Old Chan would set before them, but as the days grew longer and warmer, he could be seen sitting in the sun outside his store, thinking.

"He is deciding about The Festival of Kites," everyone would say, and sometimes he was. But more often than not, he made up small, secret poems inside his head, poems he never wrote down.

Eddie Wing could barely sleep the night before Old Chan announced this year's challenge. When he closed his eyes he saw coloured shapes drifting in his small room above the flower stall. All night long the snap of kite tails filled his ears.

Finally morning came, and as he always did, Old Chan announced his challenge.

"This year," he said, "the prize will not be for the fastest kite. It will not be for the biggest kite, or the one with the longest tail. This year the prize can only go to the kite that is smaller than any other." Then Chan sat back down to enjoy the sun and to doze. Before he slept, he made up a secret poem about tiny flying things. Unwritten, it drifted about his sleepy head before floating away forever.

At once, people began working on their kites. They bought thin cord and short, light sticks. Those who could not afford silk bought brightly coloured paper.

But Eddie did not even have the money for that. Each day he helped his parents with the flowers, and each afternoon he climbed the tallest hill in the city. There, with all the other children running behind him, he flew his dream kite.

On the day of The Festival of Kites, the sun shone and a fine, strong wind blew just as it should. With Old Chan leading the way, everyone climbed to the top of the highest hill. One by one, the people launched their kites until the sky was filled with swooping colour.

Each kite was smaller than the last. Tiny jewels of silk and paper shivered and danced in the sunlight. It seemed impossible that such delicate things could hold together in the wind, but Old Chan knew they would.

Then Chan noticed Eddie. "That boy," he said. "What is that boy doing? He is flying an invisible kite." For off a little way from everyone else ran Eddie Wing with the other children behind him.

At first all the people laughed as the boy urged his dream kite higher into the sky. Then they stopped and watched. Later on, some of them admitted to their friends that they *might* have seen something tiny and bright and clear riding high in the sky over the bay.

Old Chan knew better. He gave the prize to a girl who had flown a very small kite indeed. It was amazing that such a tiny seed of a thing could catch enough wind to fly.

But, as everyone walked back down the hill to eat and drink at the festival, Old Chan beckoned to Eddie. "Come with me," he said.

Together, they walked through the streets to the door of Chan's store. They went inside, and after much digging and moving and crinkling of paper, the old man handed Eddie Wing a parcel.

"Yours was a very tiny kite; too small to actually see. You know, you must try to do something about that."

Eddie began to open the parcel, but Old Chan stopped him. "Run along, boy: I feel a poem coming on."

When Eddie got home, he opened the parcel by himself. In the stiff, red paper lay a length of silk, some light sticks, and a ball of cord.

A few days later across the highest hill, all the children were running behind Eddie Wing once more. Now though, his kite could be seen by everyone, and it was a beautiful kite indeed.

As for Old Chan, well, he went back to his chair in the sun. In his head he made up a poem about the little boy who flew a tiny kite of dreams, a kite of air as small as a seed. But this time, before the poem could float away, Chan took up a brush and wrote it down.

AFTER YOU READ

Make a character portrait

To make a character portrait, you tell about someone by using words instead of pictures. Imagine you are Eddie. Write a character portrait of yourself. Tell who you are, where you live, what your dream is, and how you feel.

Those Tiny Bits of Beans

Written by John Weier
Illustrated by David Beyer

READING TIP

Use clues to figure out new words

Authors often try to explain difficult words by giving clues, such as a definition or a picture. As you read, note what clues this author gives to help you figure out new words.

My Oncle Henri and Tante Madeline lived in a cabin near the village of St. Jean Baptiste on the Red River in Manitoba. Times were hard. The days of the great buffalo herds had gone. People worked hard for their food and to provide their children with a good home and a future.

Tante Madeline and Oncle Henri kept a black cow for milk and a steer in the pasture and a little garden. They hunted rabbits and prairie chicken, they set nets for fish in the Red River. In winter they tended a trapline so they could make warm fur clothing.

Sometimes Oncle Henri cut and hauled cordwood along the river for one dollar fifty a wagon or helped the nearby farmers with their wheat harvest. Tante Madeline picked blueberries and saskatoons and chokecherries and cooked them into jam and preserves to store in the cellar until winter.

Oncle Henri and Tante Madeline worked hard together, in the bush and in the garden, in the cabin near the river and the village of St. Jean Baptiste. And they were mostly quite happy with each other. But one time—father loves to tell the story—they had a big disagreement. Later, when times got better, everyone laughed and agreed that it was funny.

LEARNING GOALS

You will

- find out how funny situations can happen when people don't communicate well with each other
- use clues to figure out new words

Oncle Henri didn't have many bad habits. But he did gulp his food. Every day he and Tante worked outside, and when the time came for dinner Oncle grabbed Tante Madeline's hand, he almost dragged her to the cabin.

"I'm hungry," he said.

Oncle Henri rushed into the cabin, sat down at the table, grabbed his knife and his fork, and began to eat.

"I'm always hungry. I wonder if people were ever hungry in the days of the buffalo."

Three minutes. Five minutes. Oncle Henri had very little time for doing things properly, for cutting his bannock and his potatoes. He simply gulped his food, took a big slurp of rabbit soup.

"Come," he said to Tante Madeline.

And then he was off and back to work again.

Tante Madeline knew that she and Oncle had lots of work to do: hoeing and chopping, preserving. They needed to put away food for the winter. Still, Tante was getting just a little upset with Oncle's table manners.

Why couldn't they just sit for a while over coffee, take a little time, talk about the relatives, or even the weather? It wasn't so bad at home, but Tante Madeline got especially angry when Oncle Henri ate his food so quickly at church or at school where other people could see.

One Saturday afternoon, my Tante Madeline and Oncle Henri hitched up the wagon and the two brown horses to go to a wedding. They both felt excited. Weddings were the best times. Today they would dance, and tell stories, and visit with their friends.

While they were still on the road, Tante touched Oncle on the arm and gave him a lecture on the proper way to eat.

"I'm tired," she said, "of feeling embarrassed in public. This time," she said, "this time I will help you."

Her voice sounded quite hard. Tante Madeline told Oncle Henri that she would sit beside him at the wedding. He should be careful how he ate, he should cut up his food and eat slowly.

"If you start gulping your food again," she said, "I'll nudge you under the table. Then you will stop, you'll pick up your knife and cut your food in smaller pieces."

Oncle Henri turned a little red in the face. He gripped the lines and looked straight between the horses' ears while she spoke. But he agreed. He knew Tante was a reasonable woman.

"Yes, I will do my best," he said, and he nodded.

They arrived at the wedding. Lots of guests had come. People shouted hello, and talked and laughed. They all went inside and sat down. The supper came first. Tante Madeline sat very carefully right next to Oncle Henri so she could nudge him under the table if she needed to. They all sang a song, the meal was ready to begin. And lo and behold, what did they put on the table but beans, white navy beans, with a tasty onion sauce. Those were the days on the Prairies when food was scarce, people ate a lot of beans. Potatoes and beans. Beans were sure better than starving on the Prairie.

Everyone started to eat. Oncle Henri imagined himself to be hungry again, but he remembered what his wife had said. He tried very hard to eat in a proper manner.

"The beans will make it easy," he thought, "I'll never have to cut them."

Oncle felt quite happy with himself.

The wedding was a very large one. It was so large that neither the church nor the schoolhouse were big enough. That's how weddings were back then. Family and friends of the couple had swept and decorated a big barn on somebody's farm. They put up prairie flowers and candles, ribbons and homemade paper bells. They brought in tables and spread them with huge cloths that hung halfway to the floor. When Oncle Henri and Tante Madeline sat down so carefully to eat at the table in the barn, they didn't know there was a big black and white dog sleeping under the table at their feet.

The dog didn't notice all the people sitting around
him. He was still sleeping as they began to eat. But dogs,
even black and white ones in Manitoba, get hungry too. And
when he smelled the beans and onions, this dog started to
dream. As dogs do when they dream, he began to jerk his
head and his legs. Oncle Henri felt something nudge his
foot under the table. Well, he looked up at Tante Madeline,
he was very confused. What was wrong? He had been eating
so well. Why had she nudged him? Then, he stopped eating,
picked up his knife, and started cutting his beans in two.
That's what Tante Madeline had told him to do.

Tante Madeline, when she saw her husband cutting
the beans in two, thought he was making fun of her, the
beans were already small enough.

"Ahh, now he's laughing at me," she thought.

34

She didn't know about the dog and the bump he had given Oncle's foot. Tante looked around to see if anyone was watching. She poked Oncle in the side with her elbow and glared at him very hard. Poor Oncle Henri got red in the face again. He lay down his knife. He looked up. He looked down. He tried to think, he was even more confused now. Then he took his knife and began to cut his beans even smaller.

Tante Madeline got very angry. And she got even angrier when something bumped her under the table. The black and white dog was restless. Tante got so angry that she forgot her manners and reached over to give Oncle a good thump on the shin with her heel. Of course, she didn't notice that she had thumped the old black and white dog as well.

Now in those dry days on the Prairies people hadn't learned yet how easy it was to talk things over, even sometimes in public places. Oncle Henri, when he felt the heel against his shin, took a big gulp at his tiny bits of beans. Tante Madeline saw him, by now she was red in the face too.

She pushed back her chair and took Oncle Henri by the arm. The black and white dog woke. He stretched and shook himself just as Oncle Henri and Tante Madeline stood. The table jumped. Everyone sitting nearby stopped eating and stared.

Tante Madeline and Oncle Henri were both angry and very red in the face. They looked around at all the people. Something had sure gone wrong. They hadn't fought in the bush, or in the cabin near the river and the village of St. Jean Baptiste. Why should they fight now? Maybe they should just go home. But what about the fiddle music and all the visiting? Together, they turned and marched for the door.

The black and white dog? That troublesome old dog? The smell of the beans and onions had made him very hungry. He slid from under the table, trotted past Oncle Henri and Tante Madeline, and out of the barn. In the yard he stopped to hold his nose high in the air. He stood for a minute and then started running, as if he'd seen something in the pasture.

Both Tante and Oncle saw the big black and white dog trotting across the yard. But neither realized until later the trouble that dog had caused. Tante Madeline hardly noticed him at all, she was too busy thinking of Oncle Henri. She was thinking of all the missed dances. Oncle Henri did think about the dog. He thought about the dog, about the days of the buffalo, and about hunger. He thought about rabbit stew. Oncle Henri thought the dog was probably hungry for rabbits and stew.

AFTER YOU READ

Make a list

Make a list of your new words. Beside each word, write the clue you found that helped you figure out what the word means.

Today Is Saturday

Written by Zilpha Keatley Snyder
Illustrated by Susan Todd

READING TIP

Think about your experiences

Think about your friends. What do you like about them? What do you like to do with them? As you read, see if the speakers in these two poems like the same things about their friends as you do about yours.

We started early, just as soon
As Doug had cleaned his room
And Ben had finished with his paper route.
We went the back way up to Walnut Street
And waited on the lawn 'til Mark came out.

And Mark had lots of money—birthday loot—
And he's the kind that likes to shoot the works,
And give his friends a treat.
So we went down to Gray's for Cheezy Chips
And pickles, and we sat outside along the curb to eat.
We finished up with ice cream—double dips,
With different flavours so we all could taste around.
And what we couldn't eat we gave to Jake,
That big old mutt who kind of lives downtown.
We sat there on the curb and talked awhile,
About the kind of things that we might do.

But Mark had lost his softball, and for once
We didn't feel like fishing in the slough.

So we just wandered off along the path
That starts behind the school, without a plan.
We really still weren't going anywhere,
But when we felt like running, we just ran.

The day was like that—and the things we did
Just happened. And some way, that made them seem
More special than the things we mostly do,
A little bit like something from a dream,
I guess. It was an ordinary day.
Not cloudy, but the sun was kind of dusty gold,
And never very hot.

But everything we did was fun—and no one fought
For once. We laughed a lot
At things nobody else might even see.

No one would know what it was like I guess,
But guys like Doug and Ben and Mark and me.

Writers

Written by Jean Little
Illustrated by Norm Lanting

Emily writes of poetic things
Like crocuses and hummingbirds' wings,
But I think people beat hummingbirds every time.

Emily likes to write of snow
And dawn and candlelight aglow,
But I'd rather write about me and Emily and stuff like that.

The funny thing is, I delight
To read what Emily likes to write,
And Emily says she thinks my poems are okay too.

Also, sometimes, we switch with each other.
Emily writes of a fight with her mother.
I tell about walking by the river, alone,
        —how still and golden it was.

So I can look through Emily's eyes
And she through mine. It's no surprise,
When you come right down to it, that we're friends.

I know what Emily means, you see,
And, often, Emily's halfway me …
Oh, there's just no way to make anybody else understand.

We're not a bit the same and yet,
We're closer than most people get.
There's no one word for it. We just care about each other
        the way we are supposed to.

AFTER YOU READ

Find evidence

Reread the poems carefully. Make a list of what the speakers in the poems like about their friends. Write down words or phrases each poet used to tell you this information.

41

The Rag Coat

Written and illustrated by Lauren Mills

READING TIP

Make predictions

Read the title. Look at all the illustrations. Write down three predictions about who will be in the story and what will happen.

In winter, Papa carried me into town in a burlap feed sack because I didn't have a coat. Mama, Papa, Clemmie, and me—we'd all hitch a ride on Jeremy Miller's hay wagon and huddle under Mama's big quilt. I know Papa loved that quilt, because he said it had all the nice, bright colours of the day in it, and the day was something he hardly ever saw. He worked down in the black coal mines and didn't come up till the sun was gone.

I told Papa it was warmer under that quilt than if I *had* a coat. He always laughed when I said that, and told me, "Minna, you got the right way of thinking. People only need people, and nothing else. Don't you forget that."

Papa got sick with the miner's cough and couldn't work much, so Mama stitched day and night on her quilts to try to make some money.

43

When I was old enough to start school, I couldn't go. They needed me at home to help Mama. I would card all her quilt stuffing and keep Clemmie's dirty fingers out of all that cotton. I made a doll for myself by stitching up some of Mama's quilt scraps and stuffing cotton inside. I talked to her like she was my friend, because I didn't have any. Mama was too busy for much talk, and when Papa was home he mostly stared out the window.

The summer I was eight, Papa called me over to his rocking chair. I climbed up on his lap and he said, "You're getting big, Minna."

"Too big for laps?" I asked.

"Not too big for mine," he said softly, "but too big to still be at home. It's nearing time you went to school."

I could hardly hold back my smiling just thinking about all the friends I would have. But I didn't want to leave Mama without a helper. "Papa," I said, "I can't go to school. Mama needs me here."

Papa just looked at me real steady and said, "They have books at school, Minna. You can learn things from those books that you can't learn at home."

"But I don't have a coat, Papa," I quietly reminded him.

"Minna," he said, "don't you worry about a coat. I'll think of something." But he never got the chance. Papa died that summer.

Everyone came at once and brought us food. I couldn't figure out how so many people could squeeze into our little cabin, but somehow they managed it. They all said they knew my papa well.

I sat on a stool back by the wood stove with Clemmie on my lap, so no one would step on us.

I couldn't stand it! They all wore black, black like the coal mines that killed my papa. He didn't even like black. He liked all the bright colours of the day. So why were they wearing black, I wondered.

School started in September. Mama said I could go, but I decided not to. I still didn't have a coat to wear, and I knew it was no use starting something I'd have to quit when the weather turned cold.

Other mothers who had children in school came over to quilt with Mama. I called them the Quilting Mothers.

That fall they were all working on a pattern called Joseph's
Coat of Many Colours. I looked at it and said, "That Joseph
sure was lucky to have such a coat. I wish I had one
like that."

    "Why do you say that, Minna?" Mrs. Miller asked me.

    "Because then I could go to school," I said, a little
embarrassed that I had mentioned it.

"Well now, Minna," said Mrs. Miller, "I don't know that any of us has a spare coat we could hand down to you, but I'm sure we have some scraps to spare. We could piece them together, and you'd have a coat like Joseph's after all." Mrs. Miller looked around the room, and the other mothers nodded.

Mama quickly protested. "You all need those rags for your own quilts. Don't go giving us things you need yourselves."

They paid no attention to Mama. Mrs. Hunter said, "And we could use feed bags for the inside of the coat."

My eyes filled with tears, but I wasn't embarrassed anymore. I said, "I have a feed sack Papa used to carry me in!" I ran and fetched it. "Will this do?"

Yes, it would do just fine, they told me. Then I thought of something important. "But you need to make quilts to *sell*. You can't take time out to quilt a coat."

"First things first," said Mrs. Miller, and they all repeated it. Mama smiled and shook her head, and I saw tears in her eyes, too.

The very next day I went to school, running most of the way to keep warm and thinking all the while of the coat I would soon have.

The schoolhouse was just one room filled with fourteen children. I had seen most of them before but never got the chance to talk to them much.

I knew I would love school, even though I was put in the front row with the youngest ones, and Clyde Bradshaw whispered that it was because I was dumb. Then Shane Hunter pulled my braid, and Souci Miller said I asked the teacher too many questions. But our teacher, Miss Campbell, smiled at me and said, "Smart people are those who have asked a lot of questions."

My most favourite thing about school was Sharing Day. Each of us had our own day when we shared something special with the class.

Clyde Bradshaw brought in the watch his grandpa gave him. It still ticked, and he made sure we all heard it. On her day Lottie showed us the porcelain doll her aunt from New York had sent her. We all thought it was the most beautiful thing ever and wanted to touch it, but Lottie wouldn't let anyone near it. She said, "Nope, it's mine," which made everybody mad.

I knew just what I would show when it was my Sharing Day, but I kept it a secret, and I knew the Quilting Mothers would keep it a secret, too.

Each day I hurried home to see my coat. It was looking like the colours of the fall days—the yellow-golds of the birch leaves, the silvery greys and purples of the sky, the deep greens and browns of the pines, and the rusty reds of the chimney bricks—all the colours Papa would have chosen. I decided to put a piece of his work jacket in there. It just seemed right.

The mothers worked as quickly as they could, but the cold weather was quicker. At recess Souci asked me why I didn't wear a coat. I told her I couldn't jump rope as well with one on. Jumping a lot kept me warm. I was fast becoming the best rope-jumper in the school.

Not last night but the night before
Twenty-four robbers came knocking at my door.

That was my favourite rope tune.

One night when Mama looked sad I told her things could be worse. We could have twenty-four robbers knocking at our door.

She said, "Now, what on earth would they want from *us*, Minna?"

"Oh, Mama, they would want the coat, first thing," I said.

She laughed then, but I was most serious.

Finally my coat was done. It was so beautiful, and the Quilting Mothers had finished it in time for my Sharing Day!

That morning I walked to school looking down at all the different coloured pieces of cloth in my coat. All the stories the Quilting Mothers had told me about the rags and who they belonged to, I knew by heart. I had ended up choosing the most worn pieces for my coat because the best stories went with them. I was still looking down and repeating each story to myself when I bumped into Clyde outside the schoolyard.

"Hey, Rag-Coat!" he said, and all the others laughed. Before I knew it, Souci, Lottie, and Clyde were dancing around me singing, "Rag-Coat! Rag-Coat!"

Lottie said, "Look, it's even dirty with soot!" and she poked her finger into my papa's cloth!

Then Souci said, "Hey, Minna, you were better off with *no* coat than with that old, ragged thing."

"Maybe you're right!" I yelled. "If I had *no* coat, then I never would have come to school!" I broke through their circle and ran away from them, far into the woods.

I found an old log and sat on it for a long time, too angry to cry. I just stared across the fields Papa used to gaze at.

"Oh, Papa, I wish you were here," I said, and then I couldn't help but cry. I cried for Papa, and I cried for the Quilting Mothers, who had wasted their time. I was crying so hard I rocked that old log.

Then all at once I stopped because I felt something warm and familiar. The feed bag inside my coat made me feel like Papa's arms were around me again. I could almost hear him say, "Minna, people only need people, and nothing else. Don't you forget that."

I jumped off the log, wiped the tears from my cheeks, and brushed the leaves off my coat. "I won't forget it, Papa," I said, and I headed back to school.

When I walked into the schoolroom, Miss Campbell looked up, surprised, "Why, Minna," she said, "I was told you ran home sick."

Souci jumped up, her face all red. "That's not true, Miss Campbell," she blurted out. "We lied to you. Minna left because we made fun of her old coat."

"I'll tell her, Souci," I said. "It's not an *old* coat. It's a *new* coat."

"But it's just a bunch of old rags," said Lottie.

"It is not just a bunch of old rags!" I said. "My coat is full of stories, stories about everybody here."

They all looked at me, real puzzled.

"Don't you see? These are all *your* rags!" They still seemed puzzled.

So I showed them. "Look, Shane, here is that blanket of yours that your mama's sister gave her the night you were born. The midwife said you wouldn't live but three days because you were so small. But your mama wrapped you up tight in that blanket and put you in a little box by the wood stove. And your papa kept the fire all night for three weeks. Of course, you lived, all right," I said, looking up at Shane. Shane was big. "And you hung on to that blanket for years, until it was nothing but shreds."

"My blanket," he whispered. "I thought I'd *never* see it again." He looked at his old rag like he wanted to touch it.

Then the others began discovering their old, favourite things and crowded around me. They each wanted their story told, and I remembered every one.

I even showed the piece of the woollen jacket Souci had let her calf wear when it was sick. Lottie's rag was a faded piece from the fancy dress her aunt from New York had sent for her seventh birthday. And Clyde had a scrap from the pants that he always wore when he went fishing with his grandpa.

Souci said, "Minna, I sure am sorry we ever said anything bad about your coat."

"Me, too," I heard the others murmur.

"I wouldn't blame you if you didn't let us touch it," Lottie said.

"I wouldn't blame you if you didn't want to be our friend at all!" said Clyde.

"Friends share," I said, and I let them each touch their rag. Then I showed them the feed sack inside my coat and told them how it made me feel my papa's arms again.

Shane put his hand on my shoulder and said, "Minna, I bet you got the warmest coat in school."

"Well, it took a *whole lot of people* to make it warm," I told him, and we all laughed.

AFTER YOU READ

Check your predictions

Look back at your predictions. For each one, tell what *really* happened in the story.

The Streets Are Free

Written by Kurusa

Illustrated by Monika Doppert   Translated by Karen Englander

READING TIP

Follow the order of story events

Stories usually have a series of events that lead to the main character or characters finding a solution to their problem. As you read, think about all the steps the children in this story took before their problem was solved.

Not very long ago, when Carlitos' grandfather was a boy, mountain lions roamed the hills of Venezuela.

One particular mountain was covered with forests and bushes, small creeks and dirt paths. Every morning the mist would reach down and touch the flowers and the butterflies.

On the hill above the town of Caracas, where Cheo, Carlitos, and Camila now live, there was just one house. It was a simple house, made of mud and dried leaves from sugar cane and banana plants. In the mornings, when the family went to fetch water, they often saw lions' tracks in the soft earth. Later, they would stop by the creeks to catch sardines for dinner.

Years passed and more people came from towns and villages all over Venezuela to make their homes on the mountainside. They built their houses of wood, and the children played among the trees, in the creeks, and in the open fields.

LEARNING GOALS

You will

- find out how some children worked together to make their neighbourhood a better place
- track the sequence or order of story events

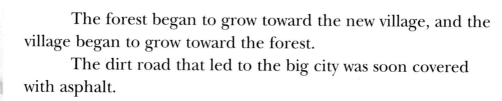

The forest began to grow toward the new village, and the village began to grow toward the forest.

The dirt road that led to the big city was soon covered with asphalt.

And more people came.

There were so many houses that they reached right to the top of the mountain where the lion tracks used to be. The creeks became sewers. The dirt paths were littered with garbage. The mountain became a very poor town called the "barrio" San José.

The children who used to play in the open fields could no longer play there, nor in the forest, nor in the streams.

55

The fields in the valleys were now filled with office towers. The whole mountain was covered with houses. The main road became a highway. There were only a few trees and not one flower.

The children had nowhere to play.

After school, Cheo, Carlitos, and Camila went to a house that had been converted into a library. There they read books, and played with clay and paints and board games and all kinds of interesting things. But they had nowhere to play hopscotch, or soccer, or baseball, or tag.

After they left the library, they played in the street.

One day, while they were playing leapfrog, a grocery truck came barrelling down the street. The driver shouted:

"Get out of the way! Let me through!"

"The streets are free," said the boys. But the truck was much bigger and more powerful than the children. So they walked to the top of the mountain to fly their kites. In about half an hour, every one of the kites was tangled in the hydro wires.

The children went back down the mountain to play ball. But the ball kept getting lost in people's washing, and trapped on rooftops.

Dejected, they went to the library. They sat down on the steps and thought.

"There must be somewhere we can play," said Camila.

"Let's go see the mayor and tell him we need somewhere to play," suggested another.

"Where does he live?" asked Carlitos, the smallest boy. The children looked at each other. Nobody knew.

"Let's go to City Hall. That can't be too far away."

"But we can't go there without adults. They won't listen to us at City Hall," said Camila, with big, sad eyes.

"Then let's ask our parents."

So the children went from house to house to ask their parents to go with them to City Hall. But their parents were ... cooking, sewing, washing, repairing, away working, in other words ... busy.

The children returned to the library steps. They just sat there, and felt very sad. Then the librarian appeared.

"Why all the sad faces?" he asked. The children told him.

"What do you want to tell the mayor?"

"We want a playground."

"Do you know where?"

"Yes," said Carlitos, "in an empty lot near the bottom of the mountain."

"Do you know what it should look like?"

"Well...."

"Why don't you come inside and discuss it?"

They talked for more than an hour. Cheo, the oldest boy, took notes on a large pad.

"Good," said the librarian, "and now what do you want to do?"

"We're still in the same boat," said Camila. "What good is a piece of paper if the adults don't go with us to see the mayor?"

"Won't they go with you?"

"They won't even listen to us," Camila said.

"Have you tried going alone?"

"Well, no."

"So, what do you want to do?"

The children looked at each other.

"Let's make a banner," said Cheo.

They all worked together and made a sign that said:

WE HAVE NOWHERE TO PLAY
WE NEED A PLAYGROUND

"Tomorrow we'll plan the details," said the librarian, and he left for the chess club.

The children put the finishing touches on their sign.

"It's perfect like this!"

They rolled up the sign and the large list with their notes.

"We're ready," they said.

Again the children looked at each other. "Why don't we go right now?" a few children said at the same time.

With the banner and the large list of notes rolled up under their arms, the children of San José walked to City Hall.

City Hall was even bigger than they had imagined. The doorway was very high. Standing in the middle of it was a big, angry man.

"We came to see the people at City Hall. We need a playground."

"But the people at the Council don't want to see you. Go home."

"Look, this is the kind of playground we want," said Carlitos innocently, and he unrolled the paper with their notes on it.

Camila said, "We need somewhere to play," and she unrolled the banner.

"Get out of here!" shouted the angry man.

"The streets are free!" Cheo shouted back, and sat down.

"We're not going to move," said another boy. "In the library they told us that City Hall is here to listen to us."

Back in San José, the mothers were worried. They couldn't find their children. Somebody said she had seen them leaving the library with some big sheets of paper.

"Oh, no," mumbled the librarian. "I think I know where they are."

The angry man in the doorway of City Hall was yelling so much that his face was turning redder and redder. A crowd gathered around City Hall to see what all the fuss was about.

Then everything happened at once. The mothers, the librarian, and the police all arrived at City Hall at the same time.

The mothers shouted, "What are you doing?"

"Take them away!" shouted the angry man to the police. "They're disturbing the peace." The police officers started pulling the children by their arms.

"Excuse me," the librarian raised one hand, "but what is going on here?"

"They won't let us talk to anyone about our playground," said Carlitos.

"The police are going to arrest them and put them in jail for their bad behaviour," said the angry man.

Then one mother, who was even bigger than he, stood in front of the children.

"Oh, no, you don't," she said. "If you put a hand on these kids, you have to arrest me, too."

"And me, too," said another mother.

"And me," shouted the rest of the mothers.

Suddenly, standing in the doorway of City Hall, was the mayor, a reporter, and a municipal engineer.

"What's going on here?" the mayor asked.

"We need a playground."

"They want to arrest us."

"Those people are starting a riot."

They were all talking at once.

"Let the children speak," the librarian suggested.

"Yes, I'd like to talk to the children," said the reporter, getting out her notebook. They told her their story.

When they were finished, the mayor turned to the municipal engineer. "Is there space for them to have a playground?"

"Yes!" the children shouted together. "We know where. We can show you."

"Why don't you come and see it?" asked the librarian.

"Um—" said the engineer.

"Uhmmmmmmm—" said the mayor.

"Tomorrow. Tomorrow we'll look at it. I don't have time now. I'm very busy. But tomorrow, tomorrow for sure. Ahem. Remember, we are here to serve you." Then the mayor shook hands with all the mothers.

"I knew it," said Camila.

"I would very much like to go with you," said the reporter. So the children, the mothers, the librarian, and the reporter all went to see the empty lot.

"What do you want the playground to look like?" the reporter asked. The children began to read their list. The reporter took lots of notes and wrote down everything on their sign.

We need a playground
with trees
and shrubs
and flower seeds
swings
an old tractor to climb on
and sticks to dig with
A house for dolls
a lasso to play cowboys
Lots of room for baseball,
volleyball and soccer,
to have races and
fly kites,
to play leapfrog, tag,
kick-the-can,
blind man's bluff
and hide and seek
grass to roll on
and do gymnastics
A patio to play on
and a bench
for our parents
to sit and visit.
        THE END

The next day, the library was empty. The children sat on the steps.

"I think," sighed Camila, "I think that nothing's going to happen."

A week passed.

One day, the librarian appeared in the doorway, smiling. He was holding a newspaper with a huge headline:

THE CHILDREN OF SAN JOSÉ TAKE ON CITY HALL

THEY ASK FOR SPECIAL PARK
THE MAYOR DOESN'T COME THROUGH

"That's us!" said Cheo.

"We're famous!" laughed Carlitos.

"Yeah, but they're still not going to do anything," said Camila.

She was wrong. The same afternoon, the mayor, the municipal engineer, and three assistants came to the barrio.

"We came to see the land for the playground. Soon we'll give it to you," they said proudly.

"Very soon," said the engineer.

"Very, very soon," smiled the mayor.

Then it happened: one morning, the assistants tied a red ribbon across the entrance to the empty lot. At twelve o'clock sharp, the mayor, dressed very elegantly and with freshly-shined shoes, came and cut the ribbon with an extra-large pair of scissors.

"I get it," said Camila, "there's an election soon, isn't there? After the big ceremony, I'll bet nothing will happen."

This time Camila was right. Weeks passed and the engineers never came back.

Carlitos, Camila, and Cheo weren't satisfied. They sat on the edge of the mountain and looked down at the empty lot and thought about it all.

Then Carlitos said, "Why can't we have a playground anyway?"

"Are you crazy? It's very complicated."

"But if everybody helped, maybe...."

It was a crazy idea, but the younger children started talking to their friends, who talked to their older brothers and sisters, who talked to their mothers, and the mothers talked to the fathers.

One day, Carlitos heard his uncle and some friends arguing about the playground. His uncle banged the table. He said they could easily build the playground themselves— they didn't need the Council. But his friends were not so sure.

"Don't be crazy. Nobody cooperates here, not even to clean up the sidewalk! How could you get everyone to build them a playground?"

"No, buddy, everyone knows each other. They'll help," said Carlitos' uncle.

"Forget it. You'll end up building it yourself."

"Alone? No. I'll help you," said one of the men.

"I will, too."

Time passed and more and more people talked about the idea. The neighbourhood committee organized a public meeting one Saturday. About fifty people came. The discussion lasted four hours and was very loud.

"We can't do it," said some.

"We can do it," said others.

There seemed no way to agree. Carlitos' uncle and the children passionately defended the idea, but most of the parents doubted it could be done without the politicians' help.

After all the shouting, there was silence. It looked like the meeting was going to end that way, until one mother remembered that she had some planks of wood she didn't need. One father said he was a carpenter. One girl timidly said, "In my house we have some rope to make a swing with."

Everybody became very enthusiastic and suddenly they all had suggestions.

"I want to bring some nails," insisted one grandmother.

Carlitos, Cheo, and Camila all started jumping up and down.

"It's really going to happen!"

All the neighbours began to build the playground. They brought cement and bricks and buckets and sheets of aluminum and sandbags and old tires and wooden boards of every size.

They nailed and hammered and dug holes and
planted and sanded. They all worked in their spare time....

On the wire fence the children put up a sign they had made themselves:

SAN JOSÉ PLAYGROUND
EVERYBODY COME
AND PLAY

AFTER YOU READ

Put story events in order

The children tried many things before they solved their problem. Make a diagram to show the sequence or order of the story events that led to the solution.

TIMES TO SHARE

In this unit, you have read about people working together to solve problems, have fun, and make dreams come true. Now it is *your* turn to work with others to make a photo essay about a special relationship—friendship.

BEFORE YOU BEGIN

Ask yourself these questions before you meet with your group:

- Do I understand the task?
- What is *my* definition of friendship?
- What should be included in a photo essay?
- Who will see the group's photo essay?
- How can I help my group to work together?

Your photo essay should include:

- a definition of friendship
- pictures from magazines, newspapers, or real photos about friendship
- a caption for each picture telling something about friendship

Make notes and bring them to your group, so you won't forget your ideas.

Remember, a group assignment always has two parts:
- the task itself
- working together as a group

MAKE A GROUP PLAN

When you meet as a group, make a plan to decide how you will work together to get your task done.

- Decide how you will take turns sharing information. You might use a system like taking turns speaking around the circle in a clockwise direction or using participation cards.

- Assign roles to your group members:
    - someone to take notes
    - someone to keep the group on task
    - someone to check noise level
    - other roles

- Review the rules for working in a group.

Participation Cards

- Everyone has the same number of cards, for example: 6.
- Each set of cards is a different colour.
- Each time you speak, put a card in the middle of the group.
- When all your cards are used, wait until everyone else has used all of their cards.

Group Member Rules

- Speak quietly.
- Take turns.
- Listen carefully.
- Stay on topic.
- Ask questions.
- Encourage everyone to participate.
- Praise each other.

QUIET!

Group Plan

- How we'll take turns:
    - Pick a number.

Roles: Angelino—takes notes
        Mishka—encourages
        Genny—checks noise level

- How we'll come to agreement:

- What we need to do:
    - Write a definition of friendship.
    - Collect pictures of friendship.
    - Write captions.
    - Put it together for sharing.

MAKE YOUR PHOTO ESSAY

1. Write a Definition of Friendship

- Use your system for taking turns.
- Listen carefully to each person's definition.
- Try to find things that are the same about each definition.
- Come to agreement about a definition and write it down.

2. Collect Pictures

- Decide how your group will collect pictures and photographs.

Angelino's group decided to find five pictures each and bring them to class.

- Share your pictures. Tell why you liked it and what it tells about friendship.

3. Select Pictures

- Choose pictures that show many different things about friendship.
- Select the pictures that best fit your definition of friendship.

Keep checking how you are working as a group.

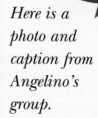

Here is a photo and caption from Angelino's group.

4. Write Captions

- Write a caption or sentence for each picture.
- Decide how you will write them. Will each of you write one? Will you write them together?
- Be sure to edit and proofread.

Friends can be any age.

REVISE AND EDIT

- Look carefully at your definition, captions, and photos. Are there ways to improve what you have done?

- Your group might share with another group to get suggestions.

- Proofread for spelling, grammar, and punctuation.

- Have you chosen the best way to share your photo essay?

Ways to Share Your Photo Essay

- a booklet
- a poster
- a bulletin board display
- a collage
- an Internet site

Think About Your Learning

As a group:

- Did we have a system for sharing information?
- Did we make and agree to a plan? Did we follow it?
- Did we follow the rules for working in a group?
- Did we check to see if everyone understood the work?
- Did we finish our task on time?
- What was our group especially good at doing together?
- What would our group need to improve the next time we work together?

As a group member:

- Did I offer ideas and suggestions?
- Did I listen carefully to others?
- Did I do my share of the work?
- What did I do well?
- What could I do better?

Unit 2: *How It Works*

Have you ever looked at something and thought, "I wonder how that works?" or "I wonder how someone ever thought of that?" In this unit, you will read about some of the items you use every day. You'll learn how they work, and how some of them were invented. You'll even have a chance to be an inventor yourself! You'll also learn about the special language that people use to share information about technology. You will

- find out about the technology you use every day
- learn reading skills to help you follow directions and understand explanations
- use diagrams, photographs, sketches, and illustrations to find information and understand how things work
- create diagrams and instructions to tell about your own inventions
- combine your own ideas with new information to extend your thinking
- write instructions for making a four-wheeled vehicle

74

The First Skateboard in the History of the World

Written by Betsy Byars
Excerpted from the autobiography The Moon and I
Illustrated by Peter Ferguson

Since none of my friends knew I was scared of anything, I was thought to be a tough little kid.

My bravery (and the rest of me) was about seven years old when I was selected by the neighbourhood to test ride The First Skateboard in the History of the World.

I didn't even know what a skateboard was. This was the summer of 1935. Skateboards hadn't been invented back then. But that did not stop our neighbourhood from making one.

Here's what went into The First Skateboard in the History of the World: one board; forty-two assorted nails; one roller skate.

77

Back then, roller skates were made out of metal and could be adjusted to stretch waaaay out for long feet, which a lot of us had. We stretched this skate out so far that it came apart. This suited us just fine. We nailed the front half of the skate to the front of the board and the back half to the back.

Then we turned the board over and hammered the tips of the nails (which had come through the board) down—hard. We had a deep respect for nails. We had all stepped on nails at one time or another, and even though we protested all the way to the doctor's office, "It wasn't rusty! I swear it wasn't rusty! If you don't believe me ask Skrunky! He'll tell you it wasn't rusty!" we still got a shot. We also had a deep respect for shots.

The whole construction took less than five minutes, and the skateboard was ready to go. By this time we knew it was a skateboard because the leader of the neighbourhood —a sixth grade girl named Bee—said, "Who wants to go first on the skateboard?"

There was a silence.

Then Bee answered her own question. "Betsy will."

There was a sort of echo from the rest, "Betsy will-ill-ill-ill-ill."

And that was how I—seven-year-old Betsy Alice Cromer—got the honour of testing The First Skateboard in the History of the World.

At the time it didn't seem like an honour, more like a military duty.

However, we always did what Bee told us to do. The explanation "Bee told me to" often made my mother explode with, "And if Bee told you to stick your head in a lion's mouth, would you?" "If Bee told you to jump off the Empire State Building, would you?" Well … I was glad it never came to those things.

We took the skateboard to the top of Magnolia Avenue, which was the street I lived on. Magnolia Avenue was not a steep hill, but the sidewalk had been buckled by the roots of old trees, and it was considered challenging for a skater.

We put the skateboard down on the sidewalk.

Bee said, "Go ahead, Betsy."

I said, "I will."

Fortunately we were unfamiliar with skateboards, and we didn't know you were supposed to stand up on them, so I sat down. Otherwise I wouldn't be alive today.

I sat, put my feet up on the skateboard, and held on to the sides with both hands.

Somebody gave me a push.

I rolled a few inches but came to a stop at the first wide crack in the sidewalk.

They pushed again—harder.

Same disappointing ride.

"This hill isn't steep enough," Bee complained, "I vote we take it to Red Hill."

"Red Hill-ill-ill-ill," came the echo.

The echo had a scary ring to it this time because Red Hill was the Alps, the Himalayas, and Mount Everest all rolled into one.

We weren't allowed to roller-skate down Red Hill. We weren't even allowed to ride our bikes down it. But nobody had told us we couldn't *skateboard* down it.

We set off in a silence tense with excitement. My throat was dry. I had recently recovered from a broken arm—the result of a daring feat on the monkey bars in Dilworth Park.

See, we had been having a contest to see who could hang on to the bars by one hand the longest, and I held on so long that my body began to angle out to the side, as if I were doing a gymnastic display of agility, which I wasn't. When I finally let go, I was horizontal to the ground and landed on my left elbow, which showed its displeasure by snapping in two. (I did win the contest, but neither of my parents congratulated me on the win.)

By the time we reached the top of Red Hill, my left arm was throbbing.

And we reached the top of Red Hill very quickly.

"Sit down," Bee said.

I didn't want to, but I had to. Bee had told me to. I sat down on the skateboard. I said, "Now don't push me till I'm ready and I'm not ready yet so don't push me till I say I'm ready, till I say 'Go.' Then when I say 'Go,' I only want Wilma to push me"—Wilma was the weak link in the gang— "and until I say 'Go,' everybody stay back and leave me—"

The neighbourhood gang heard only the "Go" and they pushed. And I went.

The first thing that happened was that all the skin was scraped off my knuckles. (I was holding onto the sides of the board and my weight in the centre of the board brought it closer to the road than anticipated.)

The next thing that happened was a three-part miracle.

The skate broke off the back of the board, the back of the board acted as a brake, and The First Skateboard in the History of the World ground to a halt twenty feet down Red Hill.

There were cries of disappointment and of determination to renail the skate and start all over again, but these cries were drowned out by my own.

"I knew it wasn't going to work! Look what it did to my fingers! If you don't know how to make skateboards, don't make skateboards! Anyway, there is no such thing as a skateboard and there never will be!"

I stormed down the hill. My shouts of outrage turned to whimpers of pain as I got out of the gang's earshot and saw the damage to my knuckles. I grew silent as I got within earshot of 915 Magnolia Avenue, my home. I liked to administer my own first-aid treatments because I was the only one who would stop administering if it hurt.

"What have you done now?" my mother asked, seeing me at the bloodied basin.

I gave my usual answer. "Nothing."

"What—have—you—done—now?" My mother always added the word *now* to give the impression that I did a lot of things.

"I went down Red Hill on a skateboard."

"A what?"

"A board with a skate on the bottom."

"I suppose Bee told you to."

Silence.

"And if Bee told you to catch a train to Timbuktu, would you?"

Probably.

So the test ride of the skateboard came and went without notice, without acclaim. I never got on another one. I never will.

But when I see kids on skateboards doing 180 ollies, ollie impossibles, lipslides, and G-turns, I think to myself, You guys would never believe it to look at me now, but I actually test rode The First Skateboard in the History of the World.

AFTER YOU READ

Look at what you read

Draw and label two pictures of the skateboard: when it was first built, and after Betsy tried to ride it down Red Hill.

On the Move

Written by Todd Mercer
Illustrated by Scot Ritchie
and Deborah Crowle

READING TIP

Think about what you know

Make a chart showing what you already know about wheels. As you read this selection and view the illustrations, think about what new information you can add to your chart.

How Wheels Work	Why Wheels Are Important

What is the single most important invention in the history of transportation? You're right—it's the wheel.

Before the invention of the wheel, people had to move things by dragging them.

BUILDING SITE
1200 KM

Some people may have used rollers made from narrow logs or round sticks before wheels were invented. They would put the rollers under the heavy object and pull or push the object forward.

But they would run out of rollers at the front of the object. So they needed to move a roller from the back to the front of the object— over and over again.

People had to find a better way to move things. The solution to the problem was the wheel.

Great Moments in Wheel History

- Around 3000 B.C.: The wheel is invented in the Middle East.
- Around 2000 B.C.: Wheels with spokes are first used.
- Around 800 B.C.: Ball bearings are invented. They allow wheels to move more easily.
- Around A.D. 1800: The first air-filled tires are used.

Wheels were fitted to chariots around 1500 B.C. Much later, the horse collar was invented. This let the horses pull heavier loads for longer distances.

How Does a Wheel Work?

The wheel is a round disk that is attached at its centre to a pole called an *axle*. The wheel is either fixed to the axle (as in a car with a motor) or free to spin (as in a toy car that's pushed).

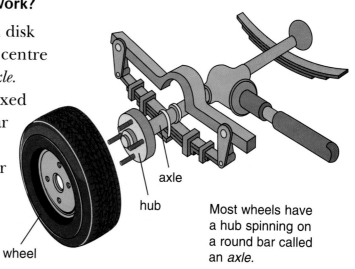

axle

hub

wheel

Most wheels have a hub spinning on a round bar called an *axle*.

Wheels All Around You

You'll find wheels at work in lots of everyday items. Wheels have been used throughout history for many interesting or unusual tools and machines.

AFTER YOU READ

Think about what you learned

Review your chart. Add any new information you learned about the wheel. Don't forget to include information from both the text and the illustrations.

Make A Water Wheel

Written by Trudee Romanek
Illustrated by Allan Moon

READING TIP

Follow instructions

Authors give directions by using action words that tell you exactly what to do. As you read, look for the action word in each step.

Not all wheels are meant to travel along a road or sidewalk. Water wheels are placed in rivers or streams where flowing water can spin them around to produce energy. Make a water wheel of your own to see just how it works.

You will need:
- a plastic 500-mL yogurt or sour cream container
- a matching lid
- scissors
- a hammer and nail
- a block of wood
- a stick, about 20 cm long
- safety goggles

1. Make a cut down one side of the plastic tub, from the top to the edge at the bottom.

2. When you reach the bottom, turn your scissors and cut 3 cm along that edge. Your cut should look like an "L."

89

3. Make a second L-shaped cut on the opposite side of the tub.
4. Make a third cut halfway between the first two.
5. Your fourth cut must be halfway between the first two on the opposite side.

> **Note:** Be sure all of your "L's" face the same way.

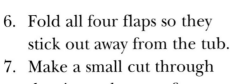

6. Fold all four flaps so they stick out away from the tub.
7. Make a small cut through the rim at the top of each fold.

8. Set the tub on the block of wood.
9. Place the point of the nail in the centre of the bottom of the tub.
10. Carefully hammer a hole in the bottom.
11. Use the hammer and nail to make a hole in the centre of the lid.

> **Caution:** Ask an adult to help you with this step, and remember to wear safety goggles.

12. Put the lid on the tub.
13. Push the stick through the hole in the lid and the hole in the bottom of the tub.

Note: You may need to make the holes larger with your scissors so that the tub can turn freely on the stick.

After your water wheel is finished, hold it sideways under running water. Does the water make it spin around? Turn it upside down and see if it still spins.

AFTER YOU READ

Make a list

Make a list of the action words that helped you follow the instructions. How else did the author make the instructions easy to follow?

Technology

Concept by John McInnes
Illustrated by Ken Phipps

Look closely at this illustration.
How many examples of
technology can you find
in this classroom?

All Around You

How Does It Work?

Written by Trudee Romanek
Illustrated by Allan Moon

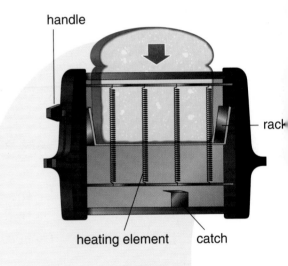

How Does Toast Pop Up?

1. You put a slice of bread in the toaster rack and push the handle down.
2. The rack and bread go down into the toaster and the heating elements come on.
3. The rack hooks onto a catch. This catch is made of a special kind of metal that bends when it gets hot.
4. The toaster gets hotter and hotter as the toast browns. The catch gets hot too, which makes it bend.

94

LEARNING GOALS

You will

- find out how some everyday items work

- use labels to figure out new words

5. By about the time the toast is done, the catch has bent enough to release the rack.

6. The rack pops up and the heating elements turn off. And you've got toast!

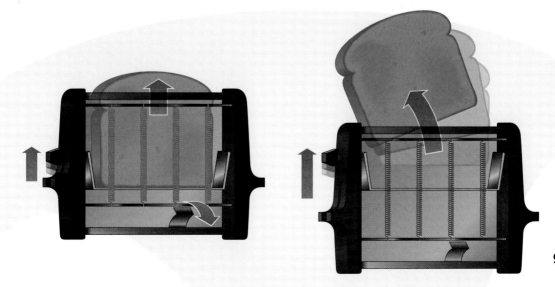

95

How Does a Key Open a Lock?

1. Inside a lock are five pins.
   Each pin is made of two
   separate pieces.

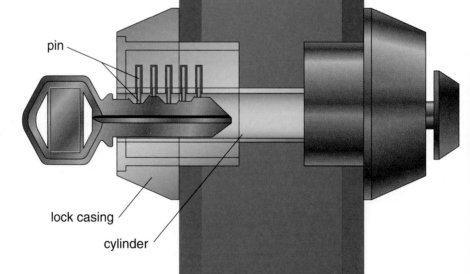

pin

lock casing

cylinder

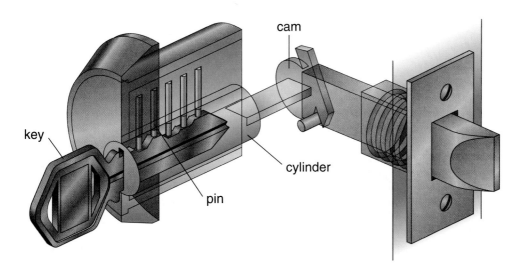

key

cam

cylinder

pin

2. When you slide the right key into the lock, the key raises the pins to the correct height. The break in each pin lines up with the edge of the cylinder.

3. When you turn the key, the cylinder turns too. Half of each pin turns inside the cylinder.

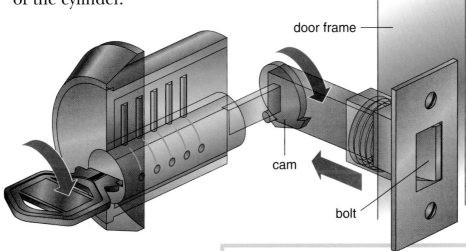

door frame

cam

bolt

4. The cylinder turns the cam.

5. The cam pulls back the bolt from the door frame.

Open sesame!

There are many different types of locks and keys. Some types have been around for over 2000 years and were used by Egyptians and other ancient civilizations.

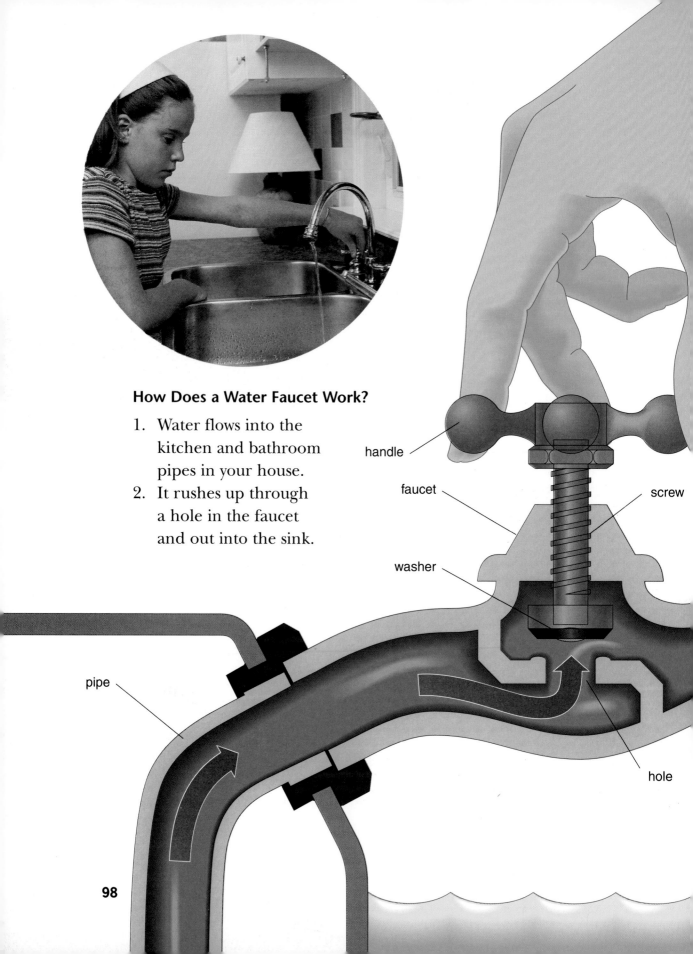

How Does a Water Faucet Work?

1. Water flows into the kitchen and bathroom pipes in your house.
2. It rushes up through a hole in the faucet and out into the sink.

handle

faucet

screw

washer

pipe

hole

3. Inside the faucet is a large screw with a plug-like washer on the end. The screw is connected to the handle of the tap.

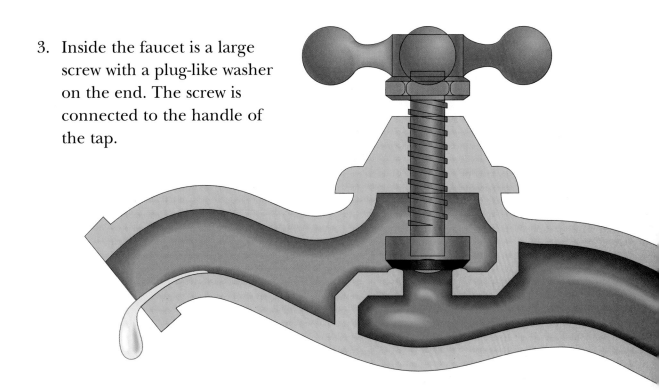

4. When you turn the handle of the tap in one direction, you push the large screw and its washer into the hole. This leaves less room for the water to come out.

5. When the handle is tight, the hole is plugged.

6. Turn the handle the other way and you lift the screw and washer up out of the hole. Then the water can flow again.

AFTER YOU READ

Make a list

Make a list of the new words you learned. Tell how the labels in the diagrams helped you understand the meaning. What else did the author do to help you understand new words?

The Lunchbox Alarm

Written by Beverly Cleary
Excerpted from the novel Dear Mr. Henshaw
Illustrated by Paul O. Zelinsky

READING TIP

Pause and sketch

When a selection has a lot of detail, it's often helpful to stop and sketch what you are reading about to make sure it is clear in your mind. As you read, stop and make sketches whenever you reach a difficult part.

Leigh Botts is a ten-year-old boy with a problem: somebody keeps stealing all the good things in his school lunchbox. Leigh's teacher assigns a project. Students must write letters asking questions of authors. So Leigh chooses to write to his favourite author, Boyd Henshaw. Soon, Leigh is writing "pretend letters" to Mr. Henshaw in his own diary.

Saturday, March 3

Today I took my lunchbox and twenty dollars to the hardware store and looked around. I found an ordinary light switch, a little battery, and a cheap doorbell. While I was looking around for the right kind of insulated wire, a man who had been watching me (boys my age always get watched when they go into stores) asked if he could help me.

He was a nice old gentleman who said, "What are you planning to make, son?" *Son.* He called me son, and my Dad calls me kid. I didn't want to tell the man, but when he looked at the things I was holding, he grinned and said, "Having trouble with your lunch, aren't you?" I nodded and said, "I'm trying to make a burglar alarm."

He said, "That's what I guessed. I've had workmen in here with the same problem."

It turned out that I needed a 6-volt lantern battery instead of the battery I had picked out. He gave me a couple of tips and, after I paid for the things, a little slap on the back and said, "Good luck, son."

I tore home with all the things I bought. First I made a sign for my door that said

Then I went to work fastening one wire from the battery to the switch and from the other side of the switch to the doorbell. Then I fastened a second wire from the battery to the doorbell. It took me a while to get it right. Then I taped the battery in one corner of the lunchbox and the doorbell in another. I stood the switch up at the back of the box and taped that in place, too.

Here I ran into a problem. I thought I could take the wire clamp meant to hold a thermos bottle inside the lunchbox lid and hook it under the switch if I reached in carefully as I closed the box. The clamp wasn't quite long enough. After some thinking and experimenting, I twisted a wire loop onto it. Then I closed the box just enough so I could get my hand inside and push the wire loop over the button on the switch before I took my hand out and closed the box.

Then I opened the box. My burglar alarm worked! That bell inside the box went off with a terrible racket that brought Mom to my door. "Leigh, what on earth is going on in there?" she shouted above the alarm.

I let her in and gave her a demonstration of my burglar alarm. She laughed and said it was a great invention. One thing was bothering me. Would my sandwich muffle the bell? Mom must have been wondering the same thing, because she suggested taping a piece of cardboard into the lid that would make a shelf for my sandwich. I did, and that worked, too.

I can't wait until Monday.

Today Mom packed my lunch carefully, and we tried the alarm to see if it still worked. It did, good and loud. When I got to school, Mr. Fridley said, "Nice to see you smiling, Leigh. You should try it more often."

I parked my lunchbox behind the partition and waited. I waited all morning for the alarm to go off. Miss Martinez asked if I had my mind on my work. I pretended I did, but all the time I was really waiting for my alarm to go off so I could dash back behind the partition and tackle the thief. When nothing happened, I began to worry. Maybe the loop had somehow slipped off the switch on the way to school.

Lunchtime came. The alarm still hadn't gone off. We all picked up our lunches and went off to the cafeteria. When I set my box on the table in front of me, I realized I had a problem, a big problem. If the loop hadn't slipped off the switch, my alarm was still triggered. I just sat there, staring at my lunchbox, not knowing what to do.

"How come you're not eating?" Barry asked with his mouth full. Barry's sandwiches are never cut in half, and he always takes a big bite out of one side to start.

Everybody at the table was looking at me. I thought about saying I wasn't hungry, but I was. I thought about taking my lunchbox out into the hall to open, but if the alarm was still triggered, there was no way I could open it quietly. Finally I thought, Here goes. I unsnapped the two fasteners on the box and held my breath as I opened the lid.

Wow! My alarm went off! The noise was so loud it startled everybody at the table including me and made everyone in the cafeteria look around. I looked up and saw Mr. Fridley grinning at me over by the garbage can. Then I turned off the alarm.

Suddenly everybody seemed to be noticing me. The principal, who always prowls around keeping an eye on things at lunchtime, came over to examine my lunchbox. He said, "That's quite an invention you have there."

"Thanks," I said, pleased that the principal seemed to like my alarm.

Some of the teachers came out of their lunchroom to see what the noise was all about. I had to give a demonstration. It seems I wasn't the only one who had things stolen from my lunch, and all the kids said they wanted lunchboxes with alarms, too, even those whose lunches were never good enough to have anything stolen. Barry said he would like an alarm like that on the door of his room at home. I began to feel like some sort of hero. Maybe I'm not so medium after all.

AFTER YOU READ

Draw a diagram

Use your sketches to make a diagram showing how
Leigh's burglar alarm worked. Include labels.

Inventors— the Problem Solvers

Written by Marc Barcza
Illustrated by Kathryn Adams

READING TIP

Read graphics

Labelled diagrams, illustrations, photos, and captions are called *graphics*. They help make information easier to understand. As you read, study the graphics carefully.

Many of the things that make your life better were invented by people trying to solve a problem. There's a person and a story behind every invention. Here are the stories of seven inventors and the problems their inventions solved.

Whitcomb L. Judson: Zipper

Whitcomb L. Judson was tired of tying his boot laces. So in 1891, this American solved the problem by inventing a new kind of fastener—the zipper. Actually, he called his invention the Hookless Fastener.

The word "zipper" was not used until 1920. The Hookless Fastener was made up of two thin metal chains that could be locked together with a metal slider. It was used for boots and shoes. In 1910, Judson came up with the C-Curity Fastener for pants and skirts.

LEARNING GOALS

You will

- read about some inventions and their inventors
- use graphics to find information

Folks didn't accept and use the zipper until around 1920, however. There were lots of problems with Judson's original invention. Early zippers often jammed or came apart. The metal used to make them wasn't very good. People actually had to take the zippers off before washing their clothes. If you didn't, the metal would rust.

Years later, a Swedish engineer named Gideon Sundback made some improvements to Judson's inventions. Sundback produced the metal zipper we know today. Like most inventions, the zipper has been improved many times. Today we have zipper designs that use plastic spirals instead of teeth. How many items can you find that use zippers?

Georges de Mestral: Velcro

Often, two inventors solve the same kind of problem in completely different ways. For example, like Whitcomb L. Judson, a Swiss engineer named Georges de Mestral created a great fastener.

In 1948, de Mestral was out walking in the woods. On returning home, he noticed seed-burs from plants sticking to his socks. As he picked off the burs, he wondered, "What makes them stick so firmly?"

To find out, de Mestral looked at the burs under a microscope. He discovered that tiny hooks made the burs stick to the loops of wool in his socks. He wondered if nature's barbed hooks could be copied and used with tiny loops to create a human-made fastener.

The loop parts were pretty easy to make by weaving thin nylon threads. But making the hooks was difficult. The solution was to cut off the tops of some of the loops to create hooks. When placed against the loops of the unclipped fabric, the hooks grabbed on and stuck with amazing strength.

Today, de Mestral's invention is used to fasten lots of things. Velcro is used on everything from clothes and shoes, to pipeline insulation, to keeping things in place on the Space Shuttle—sometimes even the astronauts themselves. Which things in your everyday life are held together with Velcro?

Wendy Murphy: WEEVAC Stretcher

Canadian Wendy Murphy is an excellent problem solver. She invented the world's first evacuation stretcher specially designed to carry babies. It is called the WEEVAC 6, because it can *evacuate,* or take away from a dangerous place, six "**wee**" babies.

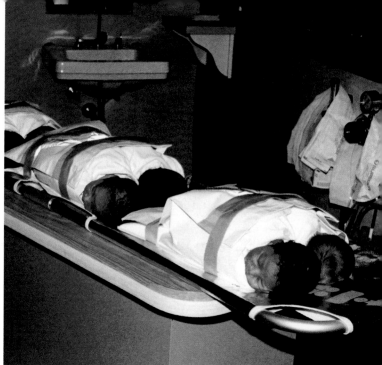

The stretcher idea came to Murphy when she was watching a TV news story about an earthquake in Mexico. She asked herself, "How can I make the evacuation process safer and quicker for infants?"

Murphy needed to know what stretchers were already being used, so she visited a local ambulance station. "I wanted to know everything about sizes. I got all the necessary measurements of stretchers, infants, and the widths of emergency exit ways."

Next, she drew a rough sketch of her stretcher idea, showing its exact measurements and important features.

Says Murphy, "After trying out many ideas and making countless improvements to my first sketch, I finally had it." Then her stretcher was tested many times to make sure it would hold up in all emergency conditions.

Wendy Murphy won many awards for her WEEVAC invention. She has gone on to invent other stretchers for adults and outdoor rescue.

Olivia Poole: Jolly Jumper

Olivia Poole's problem was how to safely exercise young babies and keep them amused. She solved this problem by inventing the Jolly Jumper, one of the world's best-known baby products.

Poole grew up on the White Earth Ojibwa Reservation in Minnesota. In her problem solving, she drew on her experience as a mother of seven children and her First Nations heritage. Poole's invention combined traditional Aboriginal and modern technology.

From her childhood, Poole remembered the cradle boards that carried infants on the White Earth Reservation. Sometimes the leather straps of the cradle boards were tied to spruce trees and the very young children could bounce up and down. This memory gave Poole important ideas for her Jolly Jumper invention.

Poole's Jolly Jumper has a harness that is hung from the ceiling or the top of a door frame. The baby sits in the harness with her feet touching the floor. In this position, she can bounce up and down, strengthening her muscles and keeping herself safely amused at the same time.

Olivia Poole and her family moved to North Vancouver, British Columbia, in the early 1950s. There she and her husband began manufacturing Jolly Jumpers. Today, about one out of every five Canadian babies uses the Jolly Jumper. As well, babies are happily bouncing in the United States, Britain, and Australia—all thanks to Olivia Poole's invention.

Kevin Joyce and Jonathan Weizman: Super Sock

Young Vancouver inventors Kevin Joyce and Jonathan Weizman had a problem … wet feet. To solve their problem, they designed a product that keeps feet dry during hiking, cycling, running, soccer, and many other outdoor activities.

Jonathan and Kevin call their incredible invention the Super Sock. How does it work? This special sock fits like a slipper over a normal sock.

The Super Sock is made of waterproof nylon, so it blocks any water that tries to seep through a shoe or boot. The result—your feet stay dry! Kevin and Jonathan displayed their Super Sock at a Canadian inventors' fair.

Maybe you, too, would like to design an invention that solves an everyday problem!

AFTER YOU READ

Compare graphics and text

Did you get more information from the graphics or the text? Give your reasons.

Disposables—To Use

Written by Elizabeth Salomons
Illustrated by Sandi Hemsworth

READING TIP

Think about what you know

Make a chart showing reasons for using and reasons against using disposable products.

For	Against

Thanks to modern technology, there are new and improved products being sold every day. When you walk into a store today, you have a lot of choice about what to buy. You have more choices than your grandparents, your parents, or even *you* did a couple of years ago!

We buy these new products because they help us do something faster, cheaper, or more easily. Many of these products are disposable. We throw them away after we've used them up. Some of the products that are designed to make our lives better may actually become a big problem for the environment.

Here are some examples of the choices you can make today.

Batteries: Disposable or Rechargeable?

Fact: Disposable batteries are cheaper to buy and give off more energy than rechargeable batteries.

Fact: It takes 50 times more energy to make a disposable battery than that battery will ever supply in energy.

Fact: A rechargeable battery can be reused for up to 10 years.

or Not to Use?

LEARNING GOALS

You will

- read how disposable products or products that we throw away affect our environment

- combine your own ideas with new information to form an opinion

Problem: Batteries are hazardous waste because they contain dangerous chemicals. When you throw out a battery, those chemicals can end up in landfill sites.

Here are some other choices:

- Use a solar-powered calculator.
- Plug in your portable music player or game player when you are at home.
- If you must use a battery-powered device, use rechargeable batteries instead of disposable ones.

Food Containers: Disposable or Reusable?

Fact: Disposable plastic and Styrofoam food containers are more hygienic than reusable glasses and dishes, which can spread germs if not correctly washed.

Fact: Disposable plastic and Styrofoam food containers save water, energy, and time because they don't have to be washed. Reusable glasses and dishes only save energy when reused hundreds of times. However, they usually break before then.

Fact: Food packaging makes up only one percent of all solid waste we throw out. Newspapers and other printed materials make up most of the solid waste.

Fact: Plastic is made from a nonrenewable resource—oil.

Problem: Although Styrofoam no longer contains harmful chemicals that damage the Earth's ozone layer, it is not biodegradable. It will still be sitting in our landfill sites 500 years from now.

Instead of adding to plastic and Styrofoam waste, you could:

- Eat at home more often instead of going to fast-food restaurants.
- Bring your own food to school or an outdoor event and keep it in reusable containers.
- If you can't bring your own lunch, take your own knife and fork and reusable glass or mug to the school cafeteria.

The Great Juice Debate

Fact: Disposable juice boxes are cheaper to make than glass bottles.

Fact: Disposable juice boxes are easier and safer to transport (by both trucks and humans) than glass bottles because they are lighter and don't break. This saves energy and creates less harmful pollution.

Problem: Glass juice bottles can be reused or recycled. Most juice boxes can't.

Can't decide which to use? Why not choose one of these ideas instead:

- Use a refillable juice container and take your own juice from home.
- Eat fruit instead of drinking juice, and drink water as your beverage.

Contact Lenses—Seeing Is Believing!

Fact: Disposable contact lenses are more convenient than reusable lenses because you don't have to clean them.

Fact: Disposable contacts cause fewer eye irritations and infections because they are more hygienic.

Fact: There is the same amount of waste in one year's supply of disposable contacts as there is in one plastic credit card.

Fact: All the packaging for disposable contacts is recyclable.

Problem: Disposable contact lenses cost about 15 times as much as reusable contacts.

Don't know which to choose? Here's an idea:

Wear your glasses as often as possible! Glasses today are lighter, stronger, and better-looking than ever. They can be safe and attractive.

AFTER YOU READ

Think about what you learned

Add any new information you learned from this selection to your chart. Write one sentence that tells your opinion about using disposable products.

HOW IT WORKS

In this unit, you have learned how to read information about technology that is presented in different ways. Information text, articles, stories, diagrams, pictures, and photographs have all been used to give information. Now you will use what you have learned to write instructions for making a four-wheeled vehicle.

BEFORE YOU BEGIN

Read all of the directions below carefully. Ask yourself these questions:

- What do I know about wheels and how they move?
- What materials do I need?
- How will I make my vehicle move?
- What do I know about writing instructions?
- How will I make my instructions clear?
- Will diagrams help?
- Who will read my instructions?

Reread the selections about wheels:

- "On the Move," p. 84
- "Make a Water Wheel," p. 88

Directions

1. Make a four-wheeled drive vehicle.
2. It must have a chassis, axles, and four wheels.
3. It must have some way to make it move.
4. Write the instructions for making your vehicle.

chassis—the frame of a vehicle

axle—a shaft on which the wheels work

MAKE NOTES ABOUT CONSTRUCTING YOUR VEHICLE

- Decide what materials you will need to make your vehicle.
- Make a list of the materials.
- Decide what tools you will need to build your vehicle.
- Write down your list of tools.

Lakshmi chose to use a milk carton for the chassis, plastic straws for axles, jar lids for wheels, and a green bamboo stick from a potted plant to push her finished vehicle. She wrote down her list of materials, and then made a list of what tools she would need.

Materials	
• milk carton (1)	• jar lids (4) (such as baby food jars)
• straws (2)	• pushing stick (1)

Lakshmi remembered to list how many of each item she needed.

Tools			
• scissors	• round tracing shape	• hammer	• safety
• pencil	• cutting pliers	• nail	goggles

Lakshmi knew she would need to include a hammer and nail to make holes in the jar lids for the straw axles.

- Construct your vehicle.
- After each step, stop and make notes to explain what you did and how you did it.
- Test your vehicle and make any needed changes.

Remember to ask for an adult's help when you use the hammer and nail.

YOUR FIRST DRAFT

1. Review Your Notes

- Gather up the notes you made while you were constructing your vehicle. Use these notes to write the first draft of your instructions.

- Write a list of materials and tools you used.

2. Write Out the Steps

- Start with the first thing you did. Make sure you tell exactly what must be done and how to do it.

Here are some of Lakshmi's steps.

1. First take an average size pencil and poke a hole in the milk carton about 1 cm away from the bottom.
2. Now do the same thing on the other side of the carton.
3. Repeat steps 1 and 2 except in the back of the car.
4. Now stick 1 straw in the pencil holes coming out the other side.
5. Repeat step 4 except in the back of the car.
6. Take a nail and hammer a hole through the lids of the jars.
7. Twist the straw so that it can go through the lids of the jars.

Remember:
- Keep your sentences short.
- Use action words, like "put," "measure," or "nail," to begin each step.
- Explain every step. Give each step a number.

If any instructions would be easier to understand with a diagram, draw one and add labels.

Here is Lakshmi's diagram.

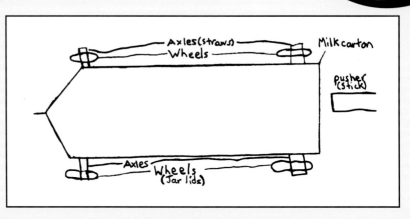

REVISE AND EDIT

- Go back and review your work. You might test your instructions on a partner. Have them do each step. Find out what extra things they needed to know and add these steps to your instructions.

- Check for errors in spelling and punctuation.

- Check that all of your numbers and measurements are accurate.

Publish It

- Plan your final copy.

- How do you want it to look?

- Where will you place the diagrams?

- Will you input your instructions on a computer, print it, or write it?

Think About Your Learning

Add your own ideas about what makes good technical writing.

- Did I include a list of tools and materials?

- Did I include exact amounts and measurements?

- Did I include every step in the right order?

- Did I use short sentences with action words?

- Did I lay my instructions out on the page in a way that is easy to follow?

Unit 3: *Stories Well Told*

What kinds of stories do you like best? What are some of the stories you like to read and listen to? In this unit, you'll read, listen to, and tell stories from many times and places. You'll find out about story characters who make you laugh, and some who make you think! You'll learn how storytellers and authors craft their work so that you can enjoy it. You will

- read stories from around the world
- think and talk about story characters, events, and ideas
- learn some tips to help you become a better reader
- find out about some of the techniques authors and storytellers use
- learn about different kinds of stories
- tell your own story

Interview with
ITAH SADU

Written by Ken Ramphal

Itah Sadu is a professional storyteller and writer. She came to Canada from Barbados. She has been telling stories since she was very young. Some of her stories have been published as books, including How the Coconut Got Its Face, Name Calling, *and* Christopher, Please Clean Up Your Room.

READING TIP

Ask questions

Make a list of what you already know about storytelling. What else would you like to know? Write down two or three questions you would like answered. As you read, look for the answers.

Itah, why do you tell stories?

Why do I tell stories? I tell stories because I believe that stories are wonderful things to bring out human emotions. I stand sometimes in front of an audience and I look at people and know I can make people laugh. The story can make people think, the story can make people remember, or it can make people feel good about themselves. You could be addressing a very serious issue and people will listen to a story about it. They will see themselves in that story. They may even cry with you in that story. So I would say I tell stories because it's a human thing to do.

Where did you start telling stories?

I grew up in Barbados, and people in the Caribbean, we're largely an oral people. We spread the news, we talk about our neighbours. There was a radio program in Barbados called "Children's Party." At "Children's Party," you were encouraged to recite your poetry, your stories, and your songs. Your parents would leave you at the radio station on a Saturday morning, and for about two hours children would gather from across the country. You would get there and you would stand and you would sing, recite, or tell stories. You were in front of a microphone and your voice was broadcast all over the nation.

Do students often ask you what gets you started on a story idea?

They do. So when children ask me that, I like to share the story called "How the Coconut Got Its Face"—I tell them that story came from a child. I took my little niece to the grocery store, we bought a coconut, and the child said to me, "What's this?" and I said to her, "Oh, it's a face on that coconut," because every coconut has a set of marks that looks like a face. And she said, "Well, whose face is it?" I told her I didn't know, and two days later she asked again and I said, "It's a monkey's face." Then and there I created the story "How the Coconut Got Its Face" for her. I saw the wonder that came into Chassie's eyes to think that her Auntie Itah could stand right there and make this thing up on the spot. And the story made sense, you know, and it's believable, and it's got a bit of magic and it's got some hope, because magic and hope are some of the elements that I include in a story.

Some people have difficulty starting a story. How do *you* start a story? Do you always start the same way?

No, now that's interesting. First of all, if I'm going to tell a story for an audience, I'm looking at a crowd of people and I'm trying to read its pulse, because as a storyteller you must establish a relationship with your audience within the first, I'd say, two minutes, three minutes. What you are having at that time is a conversation with people. And the trick with storytelling, and what most entertainers strive for, is you want people to sit there and wonder what is coming next. That's what it is. That is what separates great storytellers from the rest of them. So I get a sense of the audience, maybe it's the woman who came in late, maybe it's the little boy over there in the purple T-shirt who's dangling his legs and poking his friend. He might upset things. I need to know his name immediately. Am I going to say, "Hey good day to you, my friend in the purple. Do I have a story to tell you and your friend"? Am I going to welcome them and make them part of the beginning of my story? Yes.

And one of the wonderful things that I can do to introduce myself is to simply say "Good morning," "Bonjour," "Buenos días." Especially in Canada you can say "Good morning" in so many different languages and the audience will echo it. Then there's the traditional thing to say, "Once upon a time, a long, long time ago." Even if I were to use "Once upon a time," when was that time? Was it the year before I was born, was it the year right before Mathieu d'Acosta came with Champlain? When was it? Was it before Roberta Bondar went into space?

Itah Sadu's Tips for Storytelling

1. **Welcome your audience.**
2. **Invite them to participate.**
3. **Think about how you want them to feel.**
4. **Tell your story in your own words.**

So you find a call and response. "You're feeling good?" "We're feeling fine." "You're ready for my story?" "We're ready anytime." Just like that. And so immediately you establish yourself, you engage the audience in what's going to come next. Are you a little nervous? Is the audience nervous? Try telling yourself: "I'm dealing with human beings. I am going to tell them stories that are going to appeal to their hearts and imagination."

What about the stories themselves? Do you always tell the same story?

Stories change because of the audience. I often say to children, you will tell the same story the same way only once in your lifetime. And no two people will tell the same story the same way. Audiences make you change your stories. For example, if I were to say I'm speaking about Trinidad and Tobago, and I'm talking with grade ones, I might say this story comes from the land of Trinidad and Tobago, the land which invented the steel pan, the instrument which was invented in the 20th century. When I speak to grade fours, I might give them more details about Trinidad and Tobago. It could be about history or geography, for example.

Presentation is important. Am I going to dance my story today? Am I going to have more participation in this story today because it's for children in kindergarten?

And then it is also a question of what are the values or the morals that I'm teaching in the story and what the story is trying to convey.

What tips do you have to get students started to tell their own stories?

The first thing people always like to do is complain … talk about the things that bother them. So I say, "Think about the things that bother you.… Think about the things you like, because people also like to talk about that. Think about where you come from. What's your heritage? What's your culture? Ask your parents, "How did I get my name?"

When I put a story together, I do a number of things: I go out and I talk to people and I find out what's important to them. I talk to a woman on the bus: "What's in your world? What's in your life?" I talk to children in the playground. With your storytelling you let yourself go. Say it out loud. Say it just the way you want to tell it. Do it many times until

Itah Sadu's Tips for Story Ideas

Think about
- things you like
- things that bother you
- where you come from
- how you got your name
- your most embarrassing experience

you get it right. Think about things that are in your everyday life. Things that make you happy, feel good. Things that you want to change and ways you can change them. Things that happen to you—your most embarrassing experience or an experience you really want to share. That's your starting point—and then look at the person within you.

So look at your immediate environment, at the things that are most dear to you, that you hold precious and you start there. And the things that you wonder about, you start there. You're on your way to telling that story and try to work it orally. Be yourself. Explore language. That's very, very important. Say it in your own words. You want to tell the story like no one else in this world but you. And whatever you do, always remember that you put your best in it. A good story is a story you can tell over and over and over again. That is the essence of storytelling.

AFTER YOU READ

Think about what you learned

Look back at your questions. Think about what you learned and then make a chart.

I learned that ...	I'd like to learn more about ...

UNCLE HENRY'S DINNER GUESTS

Written by *Bénédicte Froissart*
Illustrated by *Pierre Pratt*

READING TIP

Make mind pictures

Imagine you are taking photographs of what is happening at this family dinner. As you read, imagine what each picture would look like.

Last night, Uncle Henry came to visit.

Whenever he comes to dinner, we have to be quiet, and listen to him while he talks with Mom and Dad.

I like it better when he comes to look after us in the evening. He tells us bedtime stories, but no one wants to sleep. The house turns into a ship, we become pirates, the yard is an ocean, and the neighbours, great blue whales.

Last night, Uncle Henry looked serious. He was wearing a suit and a very fancy shirt.

A shirt with chickens on it!

There were chickens all over his shirt. Yellow ones, white ones, red and orange ones. Each one was in a little square, so they wouldn't escape.

Uncle Henry had his chickens very well organized! I was wondering which seemed funnier, my uncle or his shirt, when suddenly....

On Uncle Henry's collar, a little orange chicken started to move. It curtsied to my sister, waved to my brother, then winked at me. It stretched its wings and ruffled its foot-feathers. Then it hopped down onto my uncle's stomach and started pecking at the crumbs that were there.

Uncle Henry set his fork aside, stopped talking, and scratched his stomach hard with both hands. He could not stop scratching. When you have a chicken pecking at your stomach, well, of course, it itches, it scratches, it makes you squirm! Everybody knows that; except for my mother. She said to Uncle Henry, "Now, Henry, don't start being

131

foolish!" He gave me a "for-once-I'm-being serious" look. He started scratching harder than ever. Then suddenly, he picked up his fork and became serious again … and the chicken disappeared. My sister, my brother, and I all looked at each other.

    Of course we didn't say anything. But when I saw the chicken step proudly out of Uncle Henry's plate and wipe its feet with a sly smile, I couldn't help laughing. The chicken had just laid a great big egg in the middle of his raspberry ice cream.

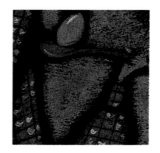

Uncle Henry asked me why I was laughing, and what kind of joke I was going to play on him now. My parents made me answer. But before I could say a word, he picked up his spoon, stuck it into his ice cream, and put it in his mouth.

He didn't see the egg sitting right on his spoon!

Suddenly, his left cheek ballooned. Uncle Henry tried to talk, but he couldn't.

When we saw his face, everyone burst out laughing. Uncle Henry tried to take out what he had in his mouth. But an orange egg is pretty slippery!

"I like your monster face!" said my little sister, and she should know, since she is the queen of monster faces. "Do another one!" But when an orange egg wants to disappear, it just goes ahead and does it!

Pretty soon, my parents got tired of Uncle Henry's monster faces. My father even said he did not like being interrupted when he was talking!

Meanwhile, the chicken had disappeared!

Suddenly, I saw the chicken on Uncle Henry's shoulder, beating its wings wildly. My brother saw it, too. He whispered, "Go get it." I didn't move a muscle. He said louder, "GO GET IT! I bet you can't even catch that chicken!"

Then he yelled, "CHICKEN ATTACK! CHICKEN ATTACK!"

At that very moment, there was a loud clucking noise, and Uncle Henry's shirt opened … and all the chickens

escaped. They looked angry. They circled over my brother.
They wanted to save the little orange chicken....

There was an explosion of colour!

Before I could turn around, red chickens, orange
chickens, yellow chickens, thousands of little chickens had
surrounded my brother.

He started waving his hands. Their feathers were
tickling him. He jumped up, then sneezed as hard as he
could. A-A-A-A-Chooooo! Ah-Ah-Ah-Ah-Shooo! Ha-Ha-Ha-
Ha-Choooom!

"He's gone and caught a cold again," my father said.
My brother sneezed so hard that the chickens went flying
everywhere. Some of them tried to hold onto the tablecloth.
They pulled it every which way.

My father was exasperated with my brother. He
slammed his hand on the table. The frightened chickens
were running everywhere....

Suddenly, Uncle Henry coughed. He whistled three notes. The chickens stopped. He snapped his fingers, and they jumped back into the squares on his shirt.

We all looked at Uncle Henry. My parents were fed up. But my sister, my brother, and I thought it was great.

Sometimes, a fancy shirt can do that. I know. Once I took a boat ride on my brother's shirt, and it was quite a trip....

But that's another story....

AFTER YOU READ

Draw your favourite part of the story

What part of the story created the best mind picture? Why? Sketch your mind picture and write a caption for it.

VILLAGE TALES-TELLER

Written by Isaac Olaleye
Illustrated by Frané Lessac

Uncle Fao Bio is the best tales-teller
In my village.
"Tell us a story," children beg,
And a wide grin spreads
Across his brown leather face.

Under the full moon and sparkling stars,
Uncle Fao Bio looks divinely happy
As he unlocks the door of our imagination
To tell us stories about Ijapa, the treacherous tortoise.

Uncle tells other stories
That fill our throats with lumps
Our minds with fear
Our eyes with tears
Our mouths with laughter
And our hearts with joy.

Go away, little tears.
Come back, glowing moon.
Come back, shining stars.
So that Uncle Fao Bio
Can fill our mouths with laughter
And our hearts with joy.

A Promise to the SUN

Written by Tololwa M. Mollel   *Illustrated by Beatriz Vidal*

READING TIP

Find out about legends

Long ago, people told stories to try to explain how things in the
world came to be. These stories are called *legends*. Think of
legends you already know. What do they explain? As you read,
find out what this legend explains.

Long ago, when the world was new, a severe drought hit
the land of the birds. The savannah turned brown, and
streams dried up. Maize plants died, and banana trees
shrivelled in the sun, their broad leaves wilting away.
Even the nearby forest grew withered and pale.

The birds held a meeting and decided to send
someone in search of rain. They drew lots to choose who
would go on the journey. And they told the Bat, their distant
cousin who was visiting, that she must draw, too. "You might
not be a bird," they said, "but for now you're one of us."
Everyone took a lot, and as luck would have it, the task fell
to the Bat.

LEARNING GOALS

You will

- read an African legend
- learn about legends

Over the trees and the mountains flew the
Bat, to the Moon. There she cried, "Earth has no
rain, Earth has no food, Earth asks for rain!"

The Moon smiled. "I can't bring rain.
My task is to wash and oil the night's face.
But you can try the Stars."

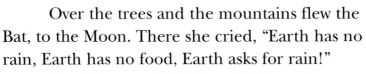

On flew the Bat, until she found the Stars at play.
"Away with you!" they snapped, angry at being interrupted.
"If you want rain, go to the Clouds!"

The Clouds were asleep but awoke at the sound of
the Bat arriving. "We can bring rain," they yawned, "but
the Winds must first blow us together, to hang over the
Earth in one big lump."

At the approach of the Bat, the Winds howled to a stop.
"We'll blow the Clouds together," they said, "but not before
the Sun has brought up steam to the sky."

As the Bat flew toward the Sun, a sudden scream shook the sky: "Stop where you are, foolish Bat, before I burn off your little wings!"

The Bat shrank back in terror, and the Sun smothered its fire in rolls of clouds. Quickly the Bat said, "Earth has no rain, Earth has no food, Earth asks for rain!"

"I'll help you," replied the Sun, "in return for a favour. After the rain falls, choose for me the greenest patch on the forest top, and build me a nest there. Then no longer will I have to journey to the horizon at the end of each day but will rest for the night in the cool and quiet of the forest."

The Bat quickly replied, "I'm only a Bat and don't know how to build nests, but the birds will happily make you one. Nothing will be easier—there are so many of them. They will do it right after the harvest, I promise—all in a day!"

And down the sky's sunlit paths the Bat flew, excited to bring the good news to the birds.

The birds readily promised to build the nest.

"The very day after the harvest," said the Sparrow.

"All in a day," said the Owl.

"A beautiful nest it'll be," said the Canary.

"With all the colours of the rainbow!" said the Peacock.

So the Sun burned down upon the earth, steam rose, Winds blew, and Clouds gathered. Then rain fell. The savannah bloomed, and streams flowed. Green and thick and tall, the forest grew until it touched the sky. Crops flourished and ripened—maize, bananas, cassava, millet, and peanuts—and the birds harvested.

The morning after the harvest, the Bat reminded the birds about the nest. Suddenly the birds were in no mood for work. All they cared about was the harvest celebrations, which were to start that night and last several days.

"I have to adorn myself," said the Peacock.

"I have to practise my flute," said the Canary.

"I have to heat up my drums," said the Owl.

"I have to help prepare the feast," said the Sparrow.

"Wait until after the celebrations," they said. "We'll do it then." But their hearts were not in it, and the Bat knew they would never build the nest.

What was she to do? A promise is a promise, she firmly believed, yet she didn't know anything about making a nest. Even if she did, how could she, all on her own, hope to make one big enough for the Sun?

The Sun set, and the Moon rose. The celebrations began. The drums throbbed, the flutes wailed, and the dancers pounded the earth with their feet. Alone with her thoughts and tired, the Bat fell fast asleep.

She awoke in a panic. The Moon had vanished, the Stars faded. Soon the Sun would rise!

Slowly, the Sun peered out over the horizon in search of the nest.

Certain the Sun was looking for her, the Bat scrambled behind a banana leaf. The Sun moved up in the sky. One of its rays glared over the leaf. With a cry of fear, the Bat fled to the forest.

But even there, she was not long at peace. There was a gust of wind, and the forest opened for a moment overhead. The Bat looked up anxiously. Peeking down at her was the Sun.

She let out a shriek and flew away.

As she flew, a cave came into view below. She dived down and quickly darted in.

There, silent and out of reach, she hid from the glare of the Sun.

She hid from the shame of a broken promise, a shame the birds did not feel.

Outside, the celebrations went on. The Owl's drums roared furiously. The Canary's flute pierced the air. And the Sparrow cheered the Peacock's wild dancing.

The Sun inched down toward the horizon. It lingered over the forest and cast one more glance at the treetops, hoping for a miracle. Then, disappointed, it began to set. The birds carried on unconcerned, the sounds of their festivities reaching into the cave.

The Bat did not stir from her hiding place that night. Nor the next day. For many days and nights she huddled in the cave. Then gradually she got up enough courage to venture out—but never in daylight! Only after sunset with Earth in the embrace of night.

Days and months and years went by, but the birds didn't build the nest. The Sun never gave up wishing, though. Every day as it set, it would linger to cast one last, hopeful glance at the forest top. Then, slowly, very slowly, it would sink away below the horizon.

Year by year the Sun continued to drag up steam, so the Winds would blow, the Clouds gather, and rain fall. It continues to do so today, hoping that the birds will one day keep their promise and build a nest among the treetops.

As for the Bat, she made a home in the cave, and there she lives to this day. Whenever it rains, though, she listens eagerly. From the dark silence of her perch, the sound of the downpour, ripening the crops and renewing the forest, is to her a magical song she wishes she could be out dancing to.

And as she listens, the trees outside sway and bow toward the cave. It is their thank-you salute to the hero who helped turn the forests green and thick and tall as the sky.

AFTER YOU READ

Write your own legend

Pick something from nature such as an animal, a tree, or thunder. Write your own legend. Use "A Promise to the Sun" and other legends you've read as models to help you write.

The Turkey Girl

Retold by Penny Pollock
Illustrated by Ed Young

READING TIP

Think about what you know

"The Turkey Girl" is a "Cinderella" story from the Zuni
people of North America. Retell to yourself "Cinderella."
Remember as many details as you can. As you read this
story, look for things that are the same in both stories.

In the days of the ancients, a young girl lived alone in
the shadow of Thunder Mountain. Her small mud-walled
hut nestled against the edge of the pueblo village, Matsaki.
The other houses rose above hers, piled atop one another,
with ladders to reach their roof doors.

The young girl was so poor she herded turkeys for
a living. The turkeys belonged to the wealthy families of
Matsaki. They valued the black-and-white tail feathers of
the huge birds for decorating prayer sticks and ceremonial
masks. The wealthy families cared little for the orphaned
herder, calling her the Turkey Girl and paying her with corn
and cast-off clothes.

Each dawn, as Sun-Father began his long journey across the sky, the Turkey Girl, clad in her tattered dress, threadbare shawl, and yucca-cactus sandals, led the turkeys from Matsaki. Ducking her head to avoid the wind-blown desert dust, she walked across a dry arroyo, through the Canyon of Cottonwoods, and up the cliff of Thunder Mountain to graze the turkeys on the flat-topped mesa.

Every evening, as Sun-Father returned to his resting place, the Turkey Girl led her beloved turkeys back to their stockade of cedar sticks.

"Good night, my friends," she would say as she latched the gate. The turkeys, although used to her talk, never replied.

The young girl faithfully tended her gabbling friends, watching over them through the hot summer and into fall, when she gathered piñon nuts from the wind-twisted pines. One evening, after she said good night to the turkeys, the young girl carried her chipped water jug to the spring. Other girls gossiped there.

The Turkey Girl knew they would not talk with her. They thought her fit company only for turkeys. She held her head high as if she did not mind. She was balancing her filled jug on her head when the herald-priest appeared on one of the flat housetops. Everyone grew quiet.

"Hear me, children of Sun-Father and Earth-Mother. In four days' time, before the harvest moon, the Dance of the Sacred Bird will be held in Hawikuh. It is fitting that you attend."

Murmurs of plans for the festival rippled through the crowd near the spring.

The Turkey Girl caught the excitement, imagining herself dancing with the others. Rich odours of the feast would rise from the fires. A pulsing beat would fill the air. Dancers in bright colours would circle together.... Water from her jug sloshed onto her tattered shawl, ending her daydream. She had no place at the dance. She was just the Turkey Girl, clad in rags.

But she could not stop dreaming of attending the dance. She spoke of little else. The turkeys were her only listeners, but they listened well, for she had always been loyal to them.

On the day of the dance, the villagers left in the crisp dawn for Hawikuh. The Turkey Girl and her turkeys left for the plains below Thunder Mountain. Tears streaked the dust on her cheeks.

As she stumbled along, a commotion among her flock drew her attention. She had no sooner turned than a huge gobbler stepped forward, stretched out his proud neck, and said, "Maiden Mother, do not water the desert with your tears. You shall go to the dance."

The young girl sank to the ground and gasped, "How is it that you speak my tongue, Old One?"

"We belong to an ancient race, Maiden Mother, and have many secrets our tall brothers do not know."

The Turkey Girl's smile brought beauty to her smudged face, "I should have understood as much," she said. "I thank you for your generous thoughts, but I cannot go to the dance. The only clothes I own are the rags you see before you."

"If you will follow us, we will tend to your clothes," replied the old gobbler, turning back toward Matsaki.

Willingly the young girl followed them straight into their pen.

"Welcome to our home," said the old turkey. Without a further word, he directed the other birds to encircle the Turkey Girl. Breaking into song, with their heads high and their wings fluttering, they danced round the young maiden, dusting her with the soft tips of their wings. Dirt and twigs fell from her black hair, which began to shine like a starlit night. Brighter still glowed her dark eyes.

Satisfied with her cleanliness, the turkeys again encircled the Turkey Girl. With their heads turned away, they fanned out their beautiful tails and entwined their wings to give her a small room in which to undress.

"Lay your clothes on the ground," said the big gobbler.

The Turkey Girl spread her tattered dress and ragged shawl on the ground next to her yucca sandals.

Swaying up and down, the turkeys treaded and tapped new life into her old clothes. They sang while they worked. Their song, a low hum, was accented with the *clack-click, clack-click* of their beaks.

Soon the Turkey Girl stood in a white doeskin dress belted with red-and-yellow cloth. Rare shells dangled from its hem. Coloured twine and beads threaded her soft white moccasins. Black-and-white turkey feathers edged her dark mantle.

As she gazed in wonder at her clothes, the gobbler spoke once more. "You must have jewels to wear to the dance."

The Turkey Girl smiled and replied, "How could that be possible, Old One?"

The gobbler tossed his head in a superior way. "Have you not noticed the carelessness of our tall brothers?" he asked. "We have collected their dropped treasures for many moons and stored them in our gullets. Now, stand still, for the time of the dance is near."

The Turkey Girl stood as still as the red-and-yellow plains beneath Thunder Mountain. The turkeys flew above her head, circling slowly, gurgling softly as they coughed up treasures. Suddenly they flew faster, and down rained turquoise necklaces and earrings of delicate beauty. Bracelets of silver tumbled after them.

"Now you may go to the dance," said the gobbler in approval. The other turkeys nodded their agreement.

"My ... my friends," stammered the girl, "how can I thank you?"

"We ask no thanks," replied the gobbler. "You have given us much. We wish to repay your kindness. All that we ask is that you not forget us. For if you do, we will understand that you are mean of spirit and deserve the hard life that is yours."

"Forget you?" answered the girl, looking down to finger her silver bracelets. "I could not."

"You will prove that by returning to us before Sun-Father returns to his sacred place."

"I will do as you ask," replied the Turkey Girl. She shifted her fine mantle from shoulder to shoulder, admiring its richness.

"And while you are gone, the latch of our cage will remain unlocked," added the gobbler.

"Why do you wish that, Old Father?" The Turkey Girl wriggled her feet, anxious to leave for the dance.

"If you break your word, we shall seek our freedom. If you return in this day's sunlight, all shall be as before."

The girl hastily agreed to his request and ran down the river path that led to Hawikuh. When she saw her reflection in the water, her excitement grew. Her beauty matched that of the desert in bloom. Now everyone would see she was fit company for more than turkeys.

When the Turkey Girl reached Hawikuh, she raced through the long covered way that led to the plaza. People were already dancing in a circle around the musicians and the altar.

The throb of drums, pulsing in the heart of the plaza, was accented with a jangling-clacking sound. Peering from behind the crowd, she saw that the sound came from the turtle-shell rattles encircling the arms and legs of the dancing braves. The sound of the rattles reminded her of the turkeys' song.

Gathering courage from this memory, she stepped forward.

The musicians, setting the rhythm with their flutes, drums, and notched sticks, missed a beat when they saw her. Her beauty was so great, everyone stopped to stare. Who was this stranger? Where had she come from?

The musicians began again and so did the dancers, although they still turned to watch the Turkey Girl. With a smile as shining as her long hair, she joined the dance.

Braves, wearing feathered masks, pressed close to dance near her. The music thrummed with power. The dancers echoed the beat with their pounding feet. Sun-coloured dust floated from the hard-packed earth. Round and round the dancers flowed like a sinuous snake as Sun-Father, high above the plaza, looked down.

The Turkey Girl danced every dance, her heart beating in time with her stomping feet. At last she was among the proud maidens and handsome braves.

But she did not forget her turkeys.

As the sun's rays slanted gold across the plaza, she said to herself, *When the music quiets, I will run to my turkey friends.*

No sooner had the music died then it sprang back to life. The Turkey Girl danced on.

Fingers of darkness reached across the plaza. *I will leave this minute,* the young girl told herself. But then a brave brushed against her, and she began to wonder how it was that she should leave the festival for mere turkeys. Were they not just gabbling birds?

In time, Sun-Father's afterglow softened the earth. Shadows of evening chilled the Turkey Girl. Her steps slowed as she remembered the turkeys' kindness to her and her promise to them. She broke from the ring of dancers, ran across the plaza, under the covered way, and down the river path to the turkey pen.

156

It stood empty, its gate creaking in loneliness.

"My friends!" cried the Turkey Girl, running through the purple of nightfall to the top of Thunder Mountain. "Wait! I am here!"

The turkeys had waited until Sun-Father fell asleep behind the mountain. Then, seeing that she had broken her trust with them, they had left Matsaki and their Maiden Mother, never to return.

Great was her sorrow at their silence. Greater still was her sorrow when she saw by moonlight that her fine dress had become rags, her shawl tatters, and her sandals worn yucca fibres. Then she understood that she had lost her turkey friends forever.

From that day unto this, turkeys have lived apart from their tall brothers, for the Turkey Girl kept not her word.

Thus shortens my story.

AFTER YOU READ

Make a comparison

Use a diagram like this to show how "The Turkey Girl" is the same as or different from "Cinderella."

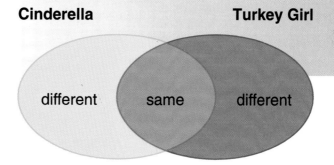

Cinderella   **Turkey Girl**

different   same   different

THE WISE OLD WOMAN

Retold by Yoshiko Uchida
Illustrated by Martin Springett

READING TIP

Stop and predict

Read the first two pages of the story. Before you turn the page, stop and predict what you think will happen next. Then read on to find out if you were right. Stop at the end of each page to make your predictions.

Long ago in the wooded hills of Japan, a young farmer and his aged mother lived in a village ruled by a cruel young lord.

"Anyone over seventy is no longer useful," the lord declared, "and must be taken into the mountains and left to die."

When the young farmer's mother reached the dreaded age, he could not bear to think of what he must do. But his mother spoke the words he could not say.

"It is time now for you to take me into the mountains," she said softly.

So, early the next morning, the farmer lifted his mother to his back and reluctantly set off up the steep mountain path.

Up and up he climbed—until the trees hid the sun, and the path was gone, until he could no longer hear the birds, but only the sound of the wind shivering through the trees.

On and on he climbed. But soon he heard his mother breaking off small twigs from the trees they passed.

"I'm marking the path for you, my son," she said, "so you will not lose your way going home."

The young farmer could bear it no longer.

"Mother, I cannot leave you behind in the mountains," he said. "We are going home together, and I will never, ever leave you."

And so, in the dark shadows of night, the farmer carried his mother back home. He dug a deep cave beneath the kitchen, and from that day, the old woman lived in this secret room, spinning and weaving. In this way two years passed, and no one in the village knew of the farmer's secret.

Then one day, three fierce warriors in full armour galloped into the small village like a sudden mountain storm.

"We come from the mighty Lord Higa to warn you," they shouted to the young lord. "When three suns have set and three moons have risen, he will come to conquer your village."

The cruel young lord was not very brave. "Please," he begged, "I will do anything if you will spare me."

"Lord Higa knows no mercy," the warriors thundered, "but he does respect a clever mind. Solve the three impossible tasks written upon this scroll and you and your village will be saved."

Then, tossing the scroll at the young lord, they galloped off as quickly as they had come.

"First, make a coil of rope out of ashes," the young lord read. "Second, run a single thread through the length of a crooked log. And third, make a drum that sounds without being beaten."

The young lord quickly gathered the six wisest people of his village and ordered them to solve the impossible tasks. They put their heads together and pondered through the night. But when the stars had vanished and the roosters began to crow, they still had no answers for the young lord.

They hurried to the village shrine and sounded
the giant bronze bell. "Help us," they pleaded to the gods.
But the gods remained silent.

They went next to seek the clever badger of the forest,
for they knew that animals are sometimes wiser than men.

"Surely, you can help us," they said eagerly.

But the badger only shook his head. "As clever as I am," he said, "I see no way to solve such impossible tasks as these."

When the six wise people returned to the young lord without any answers, he exploded in anger.

"You are all stupid fools!" he shouted, and he threw them into his darkest dungeon. Then he posted a sign in the village square offering a bag of gold to anyone who could help him.

The young farmer hurried home to tell his mother about the impossible tasks and Lord Higa's threat. "What are we to do?" he asked sadly. "We will soon be conquered by yet another cruel lord."

The old woman thought carefully and then asked her son to bring her a coil of rope, a crooked log with a hole running through the length of it, and a small hand drum. When the farmer had done as she asked, she set to work.

First, she soaked the coil of rope in salt water and dried it well. Then, setting a match to it, she let it burn. But it did not crumble. It held its shape.

"There," she said. "This is your rope of ash."

Next she put a little honey at one end of the crooked log, and at the other, she placed an ant with a silk thread tied to it. The farmer watched in amazement as the tiny ant wound its way through the hole to get to the honey, taking the silk thread with it. And the second task was done.

Finally, the old woman opened one side of the small hand drum and sealed a bumblebee inside. As the bee beat itself against the sides of the drum trying to escape, the drum sounded without being beaten. And the third task was done.

When the farmer presented the three completed tasks to the young lord, he was astonished. "Surely a young man such as you could not be wiser than the wisest people of our

village," he said. "Tell me, what person of wisdom helped you solve these impossible tasks?"

The young farmer could not lie, and he told the lord how he had kept his mother hidden for the past two years. "It is she who solved each of your tasks and saved our village from Lord Higa," he explained.

The farmer waited to be thrown into the dungeon for disobeying the lord. But instead of being angry, the young lord was silent and thoughtful.

"I have been wrong," he said at last. "Never again will I send our old people into the mountains to die. Henceforth they will be treated with respect and honour, and will share with us the wisdom of their years."

Whereupon the young lord freed everyone in his dungeon. Next he summoned the old woman and gave her three bags of gold for saving the village.

Finally he allowed the farmer to march with his finest warriors to Lord Higa's castle.

The long procession wound slowly over the mountain roads carrying its precious cargo. And it was the young farmer who carried the lord's banner fluttering high in the autumn wind.

When they presented to Lord Higa the rope of ash and the threaded log and the drum that sounded without being beaten, he stroked his chin thoughtfully.

"I see there is much wisdom in your small village," he said, "for you have solved three truly impossible tasks. Go home," he directed the young farmer, "and tell your lord that his people deserve to live in peace."

From that day on, Lord Higa never threatened the small village again. The villagers prospered, and the young farmer and his mother lived in peace and plenty for all the days of their lives.

AFTER YOU READ

Compare your predictions to the story

Tell how your predictions matched the story, using the frame below.

1. I predicted that …	**What *really* happened was …**
2. I predicted that …	**What *really* happened was …**
3. I predicted that …	**What *really* happened was …**

The Tiger's Whisker

Adapted by Sylvia Sikundar
Illustrated by Tadeusz Majewski

READING TIP

Note text features

What do you already know about how plays are written? Look through this play and make a list of the special features you see. Think about how these features will help you to read and understand the play.

List of Players

- **Tiger King**
- **Tiger Advisers 1, 2, and 3**
- **Hornbill**
- **Three more Hornbills**

- **Tiger Officers 1, 2, and 3**
- **Five more Tiger Officers**
- **Mouse Deer 1 and 2**
- **Porcupine**

The Tiger King is pacing back and forth across the stage. Three Tiger Advisers watch him.

Tiger King: I have sent tigers all over the island in search of food and they come back with nothing. What can I do? I have a responsibility to my subjects! They're going to starve. You're my advisers. What do you suggest I do?

LEARNING GOALS

You will

- read about how some small animals outsmart large and powerful enemies
- learn about special features of a play

The three Tiger Advisers converse among themselves.

Tiger King: Hurry up! I'm waiting.

Tiger Adviser 1: We must examine the facts of the matter, Your Majesty.

Tiger King: Yes? And what are they?

Tiger Adviser 2: Fact Number 1. There are very few animals left on this island for us to hunt.

Tiger King: Don't waste my time! We know that already!

Tiger Adviser 3: Fact Number 2. There are over 13 000 islands in the Indonesian archipelago, of which this island is only one.

Tiger King: What does it matter to us how many islands there are in the Indonesian archipelago? We're tigers, we can't swim to other islands. And I don't suppose the animals we hunt are going to swim to us.

Tiger Adviser 1 *(with a fake, polite laugh)*: Yes, Your Majesty, that is true. You are, as usual, right in all things. But Your Majesty is so powerful…. Why don't you command someone other than a tiger to make a reconnaissance mission to the nearby islands?

Tiger King: Yes, why don't I?

Tiger Adviser 2: Bring in the Hornbills!

Eight Tiger Officers hustle four Hornbills onto the stage.

Tiger Adviser 3: These are Hornbills, Your Majesty. May we suggest you command each one of them to fly in a different direction. The first to return with information about animals for us to hunt on another island will receive a generous reward—to be determined by Your Majesty, of course.

Tiger King: Yes, yes! That's good. *(to the Hornbills)* You've heard your instructions. There's no time to waste! My stomach is grumbling! Depart at once!

The Hornbills "fly" off on their reconnaissance mission. After a short interval, one Hornbill runs on-stage and drops onto his knees before the Tiger King.

Hornbill (*out of breath*)**:** Your Majesty, I have good news. An island not very far from here has an abundance of juicy mouse deer. They could provide food for Your Majesty and your subjects for a long time.

Tiger King: Really? (*He looks around, pleased. The Tiger Advisers and Tiger Officers express their delight.*) Where is this island?

Hornbill: Just to the east.

Tiger King: Is it the island we can see from here?

Hornbill: Yes, Your Majesty.

Tiger Adviser 1: It is close enough, Your Majesty, for us to build a bridge of stones to reach it.

Tiger King: Build the bridge immediately. My officers will carry a message to the king of that island telling him to send food to us immediately. If he refuses, we will invade the island and take what we want for ourselves.

Tiger Advisers and Tiger Officers: Yes, Your Majesty.

The Tiger Advisers and Tiger Officers lay down a series of "stones" for the bridge. To get to the island to the east, the Tiger Officers will hop along from stone to stone.

Tiger King: Is it ready?
Tiger Advisers and Tiger Officers: Yes, Your Majesty.
Tiger King: When you deliver my message, I want you to strike fear into all who listen. Take this whisker of mine with you. I want the king of the island to the east to know how great and powerful I am.

The Tiger King "plucks" one of his whiskers. The Tiger Advisers and Tiger Officers gasp, then sigh with relief when it's clear the Tiger King is not in pain.

Tiger King: Here! Take it!
Tiger Advisers and Tiger Officers: Yes, Your Majesty.

The Tiger King and Tiger Advisers exit. The three Tiger Officers make their military-style crossing to the other island with the Hornbill in the lead.

Tiger Officer 1: We're here! But I don't see any inhabitants.
Hornbill: Sssh! Here come some now!

Two Mouse Deer enter.

Mouse Deer 1 *(trying to hide her trembling)*: Hello!
Tiger Officer 1: Greetings! We bring a message from the great Tiger King of the island to the west.
Tiger Officer 2: Where is your king? We must deliver the message directly to him.

Mouse Deer 2 *(looking anxiously at Mouse Deer 1)*: We don't have a king.

Tiger Officer 3: You don't have a king?

Mouse Deer 1 *(nudging Mouse Deer 2)*: What my fellow mouse deer means is we are ruled by a queen, not a king.

Tiger Officer 3: All right. Where is your queen?

Mouse Deer 1: She's having a nap.

Tiger Officer 2: Well, wake her up! We must deliver this message to her right away. Where can we find her?

Mouse Deer 1: Our queen will be very angry if you wake her up. She doesn't like strangers. I suggest you let me take the message to her for you.

The three Tiger Officers confer among themselves.

Tiger Officer 3: All right, you may take the message to her for us.

Tiger Officer 1: This is our king's demand. Your queen must send food for all his subjects to his island immediately. If your queen refuses, our king will invade this island.

Mouse Deer 2: Oh, no!

Mouse Deer 1: I will deliver the message to our queen and bring you her answer. Rest here until I return. My friend will bring you some cool coconut milk for refreshment.

Hornbill: I'll come with you.

Mouse Deer 1: You're a bird. It will be difficult for you to run swiftly along the forest paths with me and you won't be able to see me from the air.

Hornbill: That's true.

172

Mouse Deer 1: Please be patient. I will return immediately.

Tiger Officer 2: All right. We'll wait. But return quickly with your queen's answer.

Mouse Deer 1: I will, I will. Rest in the shade of those trees. *(points off-stage)* I'll bring the answer soon.

Tiger Officer 1: Just one more thing. Our king sent this whisker to show how great and powerful he is. It is from his royal visage. Please take it to your queen along with our message.

Tiger Officer 2: We'll have a look around those rice fields while we're waiting.

The Tiger Officers give Mouse Deer 1 the whisker and with the Hornbill follow Mouse Deer 2 off-stage.

Mouse Deer 1: What am I going to do? If the king sends his army to invade our island, he will want meat. And *I'm* meat.

Porcupine enters.

Porcupine: Hello, Mouse Deer.

Mouse Deer 1: Hello, Porcupine. I'm so glad you've come. Something terrible has happened! The Tiger King from the island to the west says he will invade our island immediately if we don't send him enough food for him and all his subjects.

Porcupine: What kind of food does he want?

Mouse Deer 1: Meat! Meat! Tigers eat meat. To a tiger I'm lunch and dinner. *(brandishing the whisker)* This is the Tiger King's whisker.

Porcupine *(trembling)***:** It looks as if it came from a very large tiger.

Mouse Deer 1: It sure does. *(She shivers.)*

Porcupine: What are you going to do?

Mouse Deer 1: I don't know. At least you've got weapons. *(She looks enviously at Porcupine's quills.)* Hmmm … that gives me an idea. Will you give me one of your longest quills?

174

Porcupine: Of course. I'll help you in any way I can.
(*He reaches behind his back and pulls out his longest quill.*)
Here you go. What are you going to do with it?

Mouse Deer 1 (*measuring the quill against the whisker*)**:** You tell me, Porcupine. If this is from a great Tiger King (*holding up the whisker*), how large a creature would you say *this* is from (*holding up the quill*)?

Porcupine: A very large one! You're so clever!

Mouse Deer 1: Let me go and get rid of these three brave tigers from the island to the west.

Porcupine (*while exiting*)**:** Good luck!

Mouse Deer 2 (*running in from the opposite direction*)**:** Mouse Deer! Watch out! They're coming! They wouldn't wait any longer.

The Tiger Officers and the Hornbill enter from the same direction as Mouse Deer 2.

Tiger Officer 1: Well, Mouse Deer! Did you deliver the message?

Mouse Deer 1: Yes! Yes, I did.

Tiger Officer 2: What was your queen's response? Tell us immediately.

Mouse Deer 1: Our queen sends greetings to the Tiger King of the island to the west.

Tiger Officer 1: As she should.

Tiger Officer 2: What else did she say?

Mouse Deer 1: She regrets that she must tell you she is unable to send your king any food.

Tiger Officer 2: How dare she? Did you give her our king's whisker? Didn't she see how mighty he is?

Mouse Deer 1: Yes, of course I gave her the whisker. Our queen likes to receive presents. She also likes to give them. She would like to give this to your king in return.

176

Mouse Deer 1 hands the quill to Tiger Officer 3.

Tiger Officer 3: What's this?

Mouse Deer 1: It's one of our queen's whiskers.

Tiger Officer 2: But it's so large!

Mouse Deer 1 *(laughing)*: Our queen has many whiskers larger than that one.

The Tiger Officers and the Hornbill look at one another in fear.

Tiger Officer 1: Please excuse us. We must return to our island immediately.

Mouse Deer 2 *(very sweetly)*: Are you sure you wouldn't like some more coconut milk?

Tiger Officer 2: No! No! We're afraid not. We're in a hurry. Goodbye, Mouse Deer.

The Tiger Officers and the Hornbill exit in a hurry across the stone bridge.

Mouse Deer 1: *(laughing)* That scared them off. They won't come here again.

Mouse Deer 2: You're a genius!

AFTER YOU READ

Understand stage directions

Look at the words in italics. What kind of information does this tell you? Why do you think a play includes this kind of information?

THE RAJAH'S RICE

Adapted by David Barry
Illustrated by Donna Perrone

Once upon a time a long time ago, a girl named Chandra lived in a small village in India. Chandra loved elephants. She also loved numbers. So of course she loved all numbers to do with elephants: two tusks to polish on each elephant, eighteen toenails to clean, a hundred scrubs on a side at each bath. Chandra had many chances to think about elephant numbers because she had a special job: She was the bather of the Rajah's elephants.

Chandra liked other numbers, too. As she walked past rice paddies, muddy after the harvest, she counted the snowy egrets that flew above her.

She passed through the marketplace at the edge of the village and stopped to help the spice peddler count change.

When she joined her friends where they stood watching the Rajah's elephants parade through the town square, she remembered every elephant number she knew.

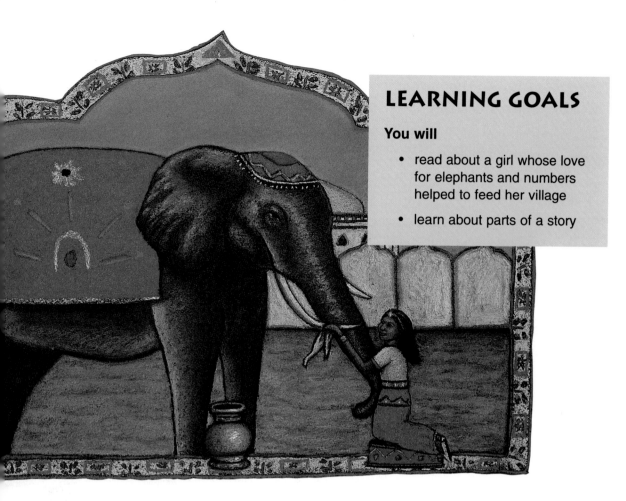

LEARNING GOALS

You will

- read about a girl whose love for elephants and numbers helped to feed her village
- learn about parts of a story

Then she started thinking about rice.

It was rent collection day, and bags bulging with rice hung from the sides of the elephants.

No wonder the people looked sad. The Rajah had taken so much rice for himself that the whole village would be hungry.

But this was the way it had always been. For thousands of years the villagers had farmed the Rajah's land. For thousands of years, he had come with his elephants to take most of the rice harvest.

The whole thing made Chandra angry, but what could she do?

On the elephants' next bath day, Chandra packed up her equipment and walked over the fields to the palace. She was about to enter the gates when the guard stopped her.

"You cannot come in this morning, Elephant Bather. The elephants have taken sick."

Chandra peered through the bamboo gate into the elephant yard. There she could see her elephants lying on the ground as still as felled trees. No amount of calling, singing, or cooing made them so much as raise their heads.

Over the days that followed Chandra sat watch over her precious elephants. She was not allowed inside, so she waited at the gate, watching medical men from all across the land come to cure the elephants.

The first doctor sat on cushions in the courtyard and feasted: he ate eight meat pastries, ten chickpea dumplings, and twelve sand lobsters served on banana leaves at each meal. While he ate, the elephants got sicker.

Another doctor spent all day and most of the night in the elephant yard chanting and burning incense. The elephants got even sicker.

Seven more doctors came and went, but the elephants got still sicker.

One morning, the Rajah returned from a walk in the gardens to find Chandra at the gate, staring in at the elephants. "What are you doing here, Elephant Bather?" he asked.

"I worry about the elephants," she said. "I love them all and know them well. Maybe I can help them."

The Rajah thought for a moment. "Go ahead and try," he said. "I need those elephants. Without them, I will not be able to carry the rice to market on market day. If you can save them, you may choose your own reward."

The guard opened the gates, and Chandra and the Rajah walked in silence to the elephant yard. Chandra approached Misha, the Rajah's favourite elephant. She studied his feet: the nails, the pads, the cuticles. She studied his tusks and the eight molars deep inside his mouth. She

studied the lips, the tongue, and the throat. She looked
deep into his eyes.

When Chandra got to the first ear, she discovered a
painful-looking infection inside the ear canal. The other ear
was the same. So were the ears of the other elephants.
Chandra cleaned their ears, sang the elephants a soothing
song, and went home.

At dawn the next day, when Chandra returned,
the elephants were walking unsteadily around their yard.
They greeted her with joyful trumpeting.

The Rajah was overjoyed. He declared a festival day
and invited everyone in the land to the palace.

The Rajah led Chandra to the ceremony room. Piled on a long table, next to the Rajah's chessboard, was a glittering array of gold necklaces, brilliant sapphires and rubies, diamond brooches, bags of gold rupees, and other treasures.

The guests began to arrive, and soon the ceremony room was crowded with villagers.

"Name your reward, Elephant Bather," said the Rajah.

Chandra looked at the beautiful jewels on the table before her. She thought about her elephants and the hundreds of sacks of rice they carried away from the village each year. And then she noticed the chessboard.

"The villagers are hungry, Rajah," she began. "All I ask for is rice. If Your Majesty pleases, place two grains of rice on the first square of this chessboard. Place four grains on the second square, eight on the next, and so on, doubling each pile of rice till the last square."

The villagers shook their heads sadly at Chandra's choice.

The Rajah was secretly delighted. A few piles of rice would certainly be far cheaper than his precious jewellery. "Honour her request," he boomed to his servants.

Two servants brought out a small bowl of rice and carefully placed two grains of rice on the first square of the board. They placed four grains on the second square. Then eight on the third square, sixteen on the fourth square, thirty-two on the fifth square, sixty-four on the sixth square, 128 on the seventh square, and finally 256 grains of rice on the eighth square at the end of the row.

Several servants snickered at Chandra's foolishness, for although the 256 grains filled the eighth square completely, they amounted to only a single teaspoon of rice.

At the first square of the second row, the servants stood awkwardly, not knowing how to count out the rice.

The next number was 512, but that was too high to count quickly, and besides, it was too many grains of rice to fit on one square of the chessboard.

Chandra started to explain, "Since you had one teaspoon of rice at the end of the first row, why not just put two teaspoons—"

But the Rajah cut in. "Just keep doubling the rice," he ordered. "You don't need to count every grain."

So the servants put two teaspoons of rice into a bowl for the first square of the second row. For the second square, they put four teaspoons of rice in the bowl. Then eight teaspoons of rice for the third square, and so continued, doubling the number of teaspoons each square.

The eighth square on the second row needed 256 teaspoons of rice, which by itself filled another bowl.

On the third row, the servants started to count by teaspoons again, but the Rajah cut in. Showing off his knowledge of mathematics, he said, "If the sixteenth square takes one bowl of rice, then the seventeenth square takes two bowls of rice. You don't need to count by teaspoons anymore."

So the servants counted by bowls. Two bowlfuls for the first square, then four, then eight, then sixteen, and so on. The rice for the last square of the third row completely filled a large wheelbarrow.

Chandra's neighbours smiled at her. "Very nice," one of them said. "This would feed my family for a whole year."

As the servants worked through the fourth row, wheelbarrow by wheelbarrow, the Rajah paced back and forth, his eyes wide in amazement. His servants gathered around him. "Shall we bring rice from your royal storehouses?" they asked.

"Of course," was the reply. "A Rajah never breaks a promise." The servants took the elephants and headed out to the first storehouse to get more rice.

By late afternoon, the Rajah had collapsed onto his couch. As his attendants fanned him with palm fronds, the servants started on the fifth row of the chessboard, and soon they were emptying entire storehouses into the courtyard.

Within several squares, rice poured from the windows of the palace and into the gardens beyond. By the middle of the fifth row, all of the Rajah's storehouses were empty.

He had run out of rice.

The Rajah struggled to his feet and ordered the rice to be loaded onto the elephants and taken to the village. Then he approached Chandra.

"Elephant Bather," he said to her, "I am out of rice and cannot fill the chessboard. Tell me what I can give you to be released from my vow."

"You can give the people of the village the land they farm, and take only as much rice as you need for yourself," answered Chandra.

The Rajah gazed at the mountains of rice that filled his palace and gardens, then out beyond the gardens to the fields the villagers farmed, stretching as far as he could see.

Then he looked back at Chandra, the elephant bather.

"It is done," he said.

That night the Rajah arrived in the village as Chandra and the other villagers prepared a celebration feast.

"Would you be so kind as to join me for a short walk, Chandra?" he asked. "I have a question for you."

As they strolled toward the village square, the Rajah spoke. "I am a very rich man, and it took all of the rice I owned to fill little more than one-half of the chessboard. How much rice would it have taken to fill the whole board?" he asked.

"If you had kept doubling the rice to the last square of the chessboard, all of India would be knee deep in rice," said Chandra, and smiled.

AFTER YOU READ

Review your predictions

Look at your chart. Put a check mark beside each piece of information that turned out to be correct. Draw a line through any information that turned out to be wrong. Add information from the story to complete the chart.

STORIES WELL TOLD

In this unit, you have learned about stories and storytellers. You have learned how to practise a story and ways to involve your audience. Now it's time to tell a story yourself!

BEFORE YOU BEGIN

Which story would you like to tell? Think and talk about choosing a story. Ask yourself these questions:

- What kinds of stories do I like to tell?
- What stories do I know well enough to tell?
- To whom will I tell my story? What kinds of stories do they like?
- What special features or effects (voices, expressions) would be fun to include?

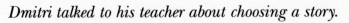

Dmitri talked to his teacher about choosing a story.

"I like to tell stories that I've known for a long time. That way I think about *how* I will tell them without worrying too much about remembering what happened."

"Our class is going to invite the kindergarten and grade one classes to listen to our stories. My story can't be too long or too hard or they will get bored."

"My favourite stories are about when someone starts out unhappy but their life is changed because they do something good. And I like stories from other countries. So I think I'll tell the story of 'The Emperor and the Kite.' The little kids will like it and it teaches them a good lesson."

PRACTISE YOUR STORY

Now that you've chosen a story, you're ready to practise, practise, practise! Here are some simple steps you can follow.

1. Learn the Story

Remember to practise telling the story in your own words.

- Read the story over two or three times. Try reading it out loud so some of the interesting words stick in your mind. Don't try to memorize it.

- Make a series of storyboards to show the main events you want to include. Don't worry about your drawing. These pictures are just to help you remember.

- Follow the order of events in your storyboards as you practise retelling your story. Practise until it is easy for you to remember the important events and when they happen.

Here is Dmitri's storyboard.

The Emperor and the Kite

This is Djeow Seow, the emperor's smallest daughter.

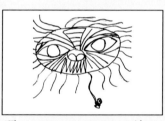

The emperor ignored her so she flies her kite when she feels lonely.

The emperor is kidnapped and put in a tower.

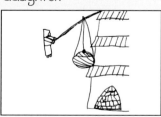

Djeow Seow brings him food in a basket on her kite.

She frees the emperor by making an escape rope that she ties to her kite.

So just remember: you can't judge people by their looks.

2. Make the Story More Interesting

- Think of an interesting way to start your story. What could you say that would cause your audience to sit up and pay attention?

- Look for places in your story where you can add
  - interesting details
  - special language
  - expression in your voice
  - actions or gestures
  - props or a costume piece, such as a hat

- Think of how you will end your story. Try to find a new twist for your ending. If you're telling a fairy tale, can you find a way to say "they lived happily ever after" in a new way?

Practise, practise, practise! Invite a friend to listen. Try taping your story and listening to yourself if you can.

Dmitri decided that he would begin his story by saying, "You might think that your family doesn't pay enough attention to you, but wait until you hear about the girl in my story!" For an ending he chose, "So just remember, you can't judge people by their looks."

3. Think About Your Introduction

Plan a way to welcome your audience and get them involved in your story. Practise speaking clearly so everyone can hear you. Think of a greeting or question to start off with.

4. Tell Your Story

- Try telling your story to a small group first.
- Try to tell your story to more than one group. The more often you tell it, the better!

Remember some of the tips that Itah Sadu gave in her interview.

Dmitri's class told their stories to small groups of kindergarten and grade one children. The children sat in a circle on the floor. The storytellers could choose whether to sit in the circle or on a chair.

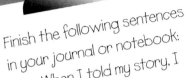

Finish the following sentences in your journal or notebook:

- When I told my story, I wanted the children to feel ...
- I hope they liked the way I ...
- When I finished telling the story, I felt ... because ...

Ways to Share Your Story

- a videotape
- a tape recording
- a presentation to your family or friends
- a class storytelling festival

Think About Your Learning

Add your own ideas to what makes a good storyteller.

- Did I speak clearly and loudly enough for everyone to hear?
- Did I have a catchy beginning to grab their attention?
- Did I describe each character?
- Did I describe where the story took place?
- Did I include the main story events?
- Did I add any other details?
- Did I use expression and gestures?

ACKNOWLEDGMENTS

Permission to reprint copyrighted material is gratefully acknowledged. Every effort has been made to trace ownership of all copyrighted material and to secure permission from copyright holders. In the event of any question arising as to the use of any material, we will be pleased to make the necessary corrections in future printings.

Photographs
Cover: John Sylvester/First Light; p. 18 (top left) Paul Barton/First Light, (bottom left) Jose L. Pelaez/First Light, (right) Don Smetzer/Tony Stone; p. 19 (top) Lori Adamski Peek/Tony Stone, (bottom left) George Disario/First Light, (bottom right) Mug Shots/First Light; pp. 70, 88-89, 91, 95, 96, 98 Dave Starrett; p. 109 courtesy of Wendy Murphy; p. 110 Dick Hemingway; p. 119 Dave Starrett; pp. 123, 126-127 Todd Ryoji

Illustrations
Cover: Todd Ryoji; pp. 6-7 Peter Yundt; pp. 8-11, 13-17 Mike Wimmer; pp. 20-27 Al Van Mil; pp. 29-30, 32, 34-36 David Beyer; pp. 38-39 Susan Todd; pp. 40-41 Norm Lanting; pp. 43-44, 46, 48, 50, 53 Lauren Mills; pp. 54-56, 59-60, 63, 65, 67-69 Monika Doppert; pp. 74-75 Stephen MacEachern; pp. 77-78, 81, 83 Peter Ferguson; pp. 84-87 Scot Ritchie and Deborah Crowle; pp. 89-90 Allan Moon; pp. 92-93 Ken Phipps; pp. 94-99 Allan Moon; pp. 102, 104-105 Paul O. Zelinsky; pp. 107-108, 110 Kathryn Adams; pp. 112-115 Sandi Hemsworth; pp. 120-121 Jackie Besteman; pp. 130-135 Pierre Pratt; pp. 136-137 Frané Lessac; pp. 139-145 Beatriz Vidal; pp. 147, 149-151, 153-154, 156 Ed Young; pp. 159-160, 162, 164 Martin Springett; pp. 167-169, 171-176 Tadeusz Majewski; pp. 179-182, 184 Donna Perrone

Text
"All the Places to Love" by Patricia MacLachlan (text), Mike Wimmer (illustrations). Copyright © 1994 by Patricia MacLachlan (text). Copyright © 1994 Mike Wimmer (illustrations). Published by HarperCollins Publishers, U.S. "The Tiny Kite of Eddie Wing" by Maxine Trottier. Published by Stoddart Publishing Co. Limited, 34 Lesmill Road, North York, ON M3B 2T6. Reprinted with permission. "Those Tiny Bits of Beans" by John Weier. Published by Winnipeg: Pemmican Publications Inc., Winnipeg, 1995. Reprinted by permission. "Today Is Saturday" by Zilpha Keatley Snyder. Copyright © 1969 Zilpha Keatley Snyder. Published by Nelson Canada, 1985. Reprinted with permission. "Writers" by Jean Little from *Hey World Here I Am* by Jean Little. Used by permission of Kids Can Press Ltd., Toronto. Text copyright © 1986 by Jean Little. "The Rag Coat" from THE RAG COAT by Lauren Mills. Copyright © 1991 by Lauren A. Mills. By permission of Little, Brown and Company. "The Streets Are Free" by Kurusa. Modified from *The Streets Are Free* © Annick Press Ltd., by Kurusa (text), Monika Doppert (illustrations). "The First Skateboard in the History of the World" by Betsy Byars. Reprinted with the permission of Simon & Schuster Books for Young Readers, an imprint of Simon & Schuster Children's Publishing Division from THE MOON AND I by Betsy Byars. Copyright © 1991 Betsy Byars. "The Lunchbox Alarm" adapted from *Dear Mr. Henshaw* by Beverly Cleary. By permission of Morrow Junior Books, a division of William Morrow &